THE
CRUELEST NIGHT

By Christopher Dobson and Ronald Payne

THE CARLOS COMPLEX

THE
CRUELEST NIGHT

by

Christopher Dobson,
John Miller and
Ronald Payne

Little, Brown and Company — Boston — Toronto

LIBRARY OF CONGRESS CATALOG CARD NO. 79-91329

FIRST AMERICAN EDITION

VB

PRINTED IN THE UNITED STATES OF AMERICA

Acknowledgments

WE BEGAN WORK on this book two years ago when Christopher Dobson, on a quiet weekend at home, came across a brief reference to the sinking with great loss of life of the *Wilhelm Gustloff*. He had never heard of this incident before. Neither had Ronald Payne, with whom he had recently worked on their study of terrorism, *The Carlos Complex*.

Together they began probing the subject and discovered that two German liners in the great evacuation over the Baltic Sea in 1945 had been sunk by the same Soviet submarine commander, Captain Marinesko. It was at this point that they consulted John Miller, an old Moscow hand and writer on foreign affairs for the *Daily Telegraph*. He was about to leave for Moscow on a *Telegraph* assignment and promised to find out more about the Soviet submarine ace.

When he returned he reproached Dobson and Payne. "Official Russians warned me off the subject," he complained. For it appeared that Marinesko had been involved in political scandal, and Miller's questions were not welcomed. In further visits to the Soviet capital he unearthed a great deal of new material about this Russian hero who for more than twenty years had been an "unperson".

Meanwhile Dobson and Payne were in touch with the Imperial War Museum, to whom our thanks are due for their help and interest, and were researching in West German archives. We are particularly grateful to Professor Jürgen Rohwer, the distinguished German historian of the war at sea, who on several occasions pointed us in the right direction. At home Captain Stephen Roskill, R.N., was also kind enough to give his advice.

While in West Germany, Payne received much help from

5

Captain Kurt Reitsch, formerly of the German Navy, and from his wife, Wilhelmina, who served during the war in the Women's Naval Auxiliaries. They kindly accompanied him on a visit to Gross Admiral Karl Doenitz, who was responsible for the seaborne evacuation of which the *Wilhelm Gustloff* was a part. We should like to acknowledge the friendly interest which the Admiral took in our enterprise and also to thank Captain Reitsch and his wife for helping with the most difficult part of the enterprise, the tracking down of survivors thirty-three years after the event.

To the survivors themselves who were willing to rehearse for our benefit memories of a terrible experience we express our warmest thanks. In Hamburg, Baroness Ebbi von Maydell and her son Gunther, both of whom survived the sinking, went to great trouble to give us a complete account both of their own experiences and of those of their friend Professor Bock, who died in 1976.

Frau Paula Maria Graf in the Rhineland was also more than kind in putting us in touch with her former husband Herr Walter Knust in Hamburg and in telling her own painful story. We also interviewed Heinz Schoen, himself the author of a remarkable book on the *Gustloff* and a survivor of the tragedy.

For help in discovering what it was like to be in the Bay of Danzig in 1945 we are beholden to Fritz Brustat-Naval, a former naval officer who wrote a vivid book about the sea evacuation and told us a good deal about those involved. We are indebted for similar help to Commander Hugo Heydel, a retired officer who served in the area. We were also impressed by the succinct account of naval headquarters' disputes before the *Gustloff* sailed given by Cajus Bekker in his book *Flucht übers Meer* and should like to acknowledge our debt to him in this regard.

Great assistance was also given by Alfred de Zayas, head of an American research team at the University of Göttingen and author of *Nemesis at Potsdam*. He introduced us to Countess zu Eulenberg and her husband, Colonel Count Carl

6

zu Eulenberg, who recounted for us their wartime experiences, as did Hildegard Schneider, who had been an army nurse.

We should like to express our thanks to Hans Jurgen Witthöft of the press department of Hapag-Lloyd in Hamburg, and to Blohm & Voss who sent us plans and details of the *Wilhelm Gustloff*. We are also greatly indebted to Gunther Molter of Mercedes Benz, whose generosity in putting a car at our disposal made our travels in West Germany a pleasure.

John England, Bonn correspondent of the *Sunday Telegraph*, gave us unflappable moral support. A young Hamburg student, Christian Wieg, interpreted at interviews and wholeheartedly shared our enthusiasm in the quest.

Gertrud Fraser, who experienced the horrors of the German withdrawal from Moscow and now lives in London, gave us help with the translation of German material. Mrs. Kira Miller helped with Russian technical translations. Adrian Secker of the *Financial Times* made many valuable comments. Andrea Whittaker was an attractive and expert "crash" translator.

These acknowledgments would not be complete without mention of the constant help of Peter Brightman, the most enthusiastic bloodhound in the research business.

Finally we would like to pay tribute to a handful of Soviet patriots who pointed the way over documenting the rise and fall of the brave and tragic Captain Marinesko.

Readers familiar with censorship in the Soviet Union will appreciate that Soviet heroes can only be whiter than white, and any book published in the West about one of them is almost certainly going to be unacceptable. Nevertheless we are grateful for advice from Mr. Mikhail Fatayev, Director of the Leningrad Central Naval Museum, officials of the Central Naval Archives in Gatchina, the Soviet Committee of War Veterans, and the Union of Writers.

Others have wanted the full story told because they felt it

reflected credit on the courage and resourcefulness of a real Soviet man, and was also a powerful reminder of the horrors and futility of war. We salute these people, and because we know they would not want us to mention their names or define their contribution we will leave it at that. We hope that the result will justify their courage and the help that everyone else has given us.

Illustrations

Photographs follow page 96

Admiral Doenitz
Launching the *Wilhelm Gustloff*
Shipboard views of the *Wilhelm Gustloff*
The German cruise liner in peacetime
Frau Paula Knust and her boarding pass and certificate
of rescue
Professor Bock in his cabin
The S 13 loading torpedoes
Gauleiter Erich Koch
Captain Alexander Marinesko
Captain Lieutenant Nikolai Redkoborodov

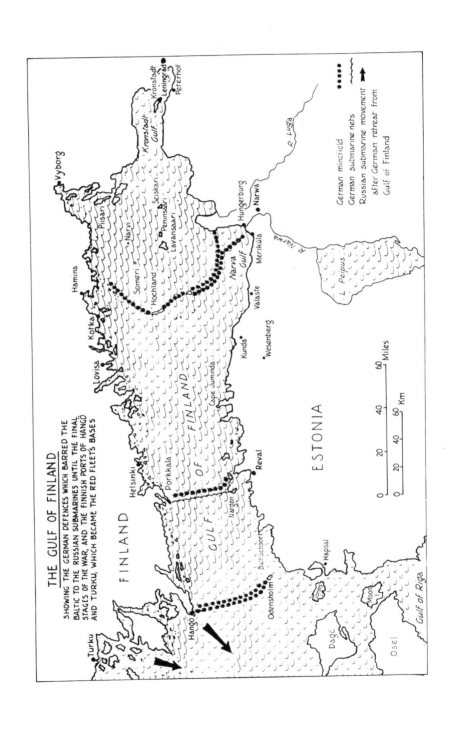

THE GULF OF FINLAND

SHOWING THE GERMAN DEFENCES WHICH BARRED THE
BALTIC TO THE RUSSIAN SUBMARINES UNTIL THE FINAL
STAGES OF THE WAR, AND THE FINNISH PORTS OF HANGÖ
AND TURKU, WHICH BECAME THE RED FLEET'S BASES

German minefield

German submarine nets

Russian submarine movement
after German retreat from
Gulf of Finland

FINLAND

Turku

Hangö

Odensholm

Baltischport

Porkkala

Helsinki

Nargön

Reval

Hapsal

Dagö

Osel

Moon

Gulf of Riga

ESTONIA

Cape Juminda

Kunda

Wesenberg

Valaste

Merikula

Narva Gulf

Hungerburg

Narwa

L. Peipus

R. NARWA

R. Luga

Lovisa

Kotka

Hamina

Hochland

Lavansaari

Peninssari

Seiskari

Piisari

Narvi

Someri

Vyborg

Kronstadt
Gulf

Kronstadt

Leningrad

Peterhof

GULF   OF   FINLAND

Miles
0   20   40   60

Km
0   20   40   60

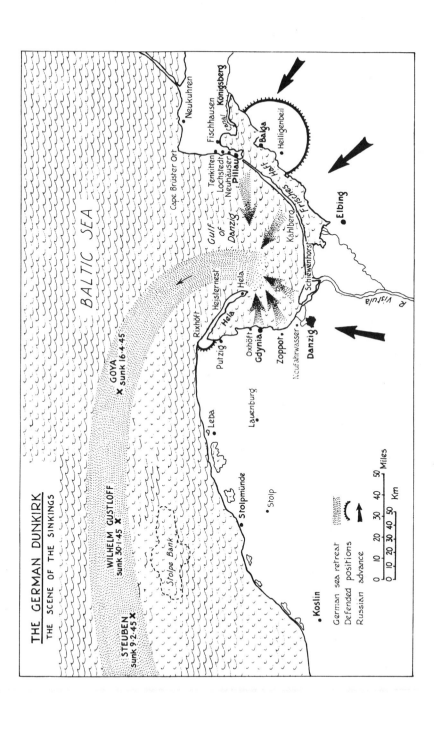

THE GERMAN DUNKIRK
THE SCENE OF THE SINKINGS

BALTIC SEA

STEUBEN
Sunk 9·2·45 ✗

WILHELM GUSTLOFF ✗
Sunk 30·1·45

GOYA
✗ Sunk 16·4·45

Stolpe Bank

Koslin

Stolp

Stolpmünde

Leba

Lauenburg

Putzig

Rixhöft

Heisternest

Hela

Oxhöft

Gdynia

Zoppot

Danzig

Neufahrwasser

Schiewenhorst

R. Vistula

Kahlberg

Frisches Haff

Gulf of Danzig

Cape Brüster Ort

Neukuhren

Fischhausen

Königsberg

Canal

Tenkitten

Lochstedt

Neuhäuser

Pillau

Balga

Heiligenbeil

Elbing

German sea retreat
Defended positions
Russian advance

0   10   20   30   40   50 Miles
0 10 20 30 40 50 Km

I

ON THE FREEZING night of January 30th, 1945, the German liner *Wilhelm Gustloff* heaved her 25,484 tons through the stiff chop of the Baltic Sea. Ice formed on her decks. Flurries of snow blotted out the fitful moon. Her look-outs, numb with cold, could see little beyond the bulk of the ship. Below decks, most of her passengers were seasick.

The *Wilhelm Gustloff* was not a good heavy-weather boat. She had been built as a cruise ship for calmer, sunnier waters than these. Her complement, in normal times, was a crew of 400 to serve 1,465 passengers who, even if not accommodated in the lavish style of the great Atlantic liners, still enjoyed conditions of relaxed comfort.

But these were not normal times, and the *Wilhelm Gustloff* was on no pleasure cruise. The war was in its last year. Germany, though facing inevitable defeat, was still fighting desperate rearguard actions on all fronts. And the time had come for Germany's own "Dunkirk".

Millions of refugees, panic-stricken as the avenging Russian armies pressed remorselessly westward, had poured into the German-held ports of the Baltic Sea. To those ports came the ambulance trains loaded with German soldiers wounded in the great battles in the East. And in those ports, too, were some thousands of men essential to Germany's capacity to continue the war at sea – highly trained submarine crews and naval specialists of various kinds.

For all, the unthinkable fate was to fall into the hands of the Russians; and for all, there was only one practical way of escape. That was by sea. Land transport facilities to cope with that number just did not exist. Roads and railways were constantly being cut by fresh Russian advances.

Therefore the German High Command decided on a massive evacuation over the water. It received little publicity at the time, being overshadowed by the climactic battles on land, and it has been largely ignored since. But it was a stupendous operation. Between January 23rd and May 8th, 1945, the German Navy and Merchant Navy, using everything from liners to trawlers, operating virtually without air cover and with surface escorts of derisory proportions, lifted no fewer than 2,022,602 refugees and soldiers beyond the reach of the Red Army.

It was to play her role in that operation that the *Wilhelm Gustloff* sailed from Gdynia, near Danzig, on the morning of January 30th. It was for that reason that instead of her normal complement of nearly 1,900, she had *no fewer than 8,000 people on board*. She was refugee ship, and troop transport, and hospital ship.

The constant traffic of German ships across the Baltic had not, of course, gone unchallenged. The main threat to the hastily-improvised, scantily-protected convoys came from Russian submarines which, for most of the war, had not had great success in those waters. Now came their chance to strike.

As the *Wilhelm Gustloff* thrust her way through the choppy, ice-cold sea, she was spotted and shadowed by the Russian submarine S 13, commanded by Captain Third Class (Commander) Alexander Marinesko, a rumbustious character of the type found in all navies: a womaniser, a hard drinker, a rebel against some forms of discipline, but a brilliant submarine commander.

When Marinesko trained his periscope on the former German cruise liner, the scene was set for a sea disaster on a monumental scale.

When loss of life at sea is under discussion, the first name that springs to mind is inevitably that of the *Titanic*, the White Star liner which hit an iceberg in the Atlantic on her maiden voyage. Then comes, for most people, the *Lusitania*, sunk by the Germans in the First World War; to be followed perhaps by the *Athenia*, torpedoed in the opening hours of the Second World War, or the Italian liner, *Andrea Doria*, sunk in a collision off New York, or the Canadian Pacific Line's *Empress of Ireland*, victim of a collision in the St. Lawrence estuary with horrifying casualty figures.

No one ever speaks of the *Wilhelm Gustloff*. Indeed, few people – outside Germany, at least – have even heard of her.

Yet the death toll in the *Wilhelm Gustloff* disaster was five times as great as that in the *Titanic*, and more than that in all the ships listed above put together – the *Titanic* included.

It is almost incredible that a calamity of such proportions should have attracted so little attention, particularly as the *Wilhelm Gustloff* was a ship which had unique associations with the New Germany which Hitler established in the 1930s.

It is equally remarkable that the massive maritime enterprise in which she met her end should have rated little more than a footnote in most war histories.

To understand the story of the ship that no one has heard of, and to grasp the motivation behind her last voyage, it is necessary, first, to consider what happened in a certain village in 1944; a town with a name which, to most people, is just as unfamiliar as that of the *Wilhelm Gustloff* herself.

The name of the town is Nemmersdorf.

2

NEMMERSDORF IS NOT a seaport. It is an inland town, situated just inside East Prussia's wartime border with Poland. On October 22nd, 1944, when the westward drive of the Red Army was gaining momentum, Nemmersdorf had the misfortune to be the first place in Germany proper to fall into Russian hands. It was overrun by General Galitsky's 11th Guards Army.

It was natural enough that Russian soldiers who had seen their own families slaughtered and their own homes and crops burned should have scores to settle with the "Fritzes". Nemmersdorf was where the terrible settlement began.

Russian propagandists exhorted the troops to "kill all the Fascists", and discipline was deliberately relaxed. Without precisely commanding it, the Russian army restored the medieval military order of "rape and pillage" by letting the soldiers know that rape, a crime punishable by death inside the Soviet Union, was to be enjoyed the moment they crossed the border. It was, according to Alexander Solzhenitsyn, "a combat distinction". In addition, the soldiers were allowed to send home by post anything they had looted but could not carry with them. And so rape, killing and looting were indulged in with such ferocity that eventually discipline had to be restored in some areas in order to force the soldiers back to the serious business of fighting the war.

Five days after the Russians occupied Nemmersdorf, General Friedrich Hossbach and his battered Fourth Army threw them out again. When his troops arrived in the village, hardly a single inhabitant remained alive. Women had been nailed to barn doors and farm carts, tanks had crushed those who had tried to flee, children had been shot.

16

The Russian killing had been indiscriminate. Forty French prisoners of war who welcomed them as liberators were shot as spies. So were German Communists who had waited so long for their comrades to arrive and were foolhardy enough to greet them with bread and salt and praise for the Soviet Union.

It was as though Nemmersdorf had been visited by an army of savages, with the bodies of men and the minds of cruel children. It was not the organised butchery practised by the German execution squads in occupied territory, though the results were similar. It was the casual brutality of soldiers from whom the restraints of discipline had been deliberately lifted. Major Lev Kopelev, an ardent Communist, whose task was to subvert and indoctrinate the Germans – he had talked one German garrison into mutinying – was arrested by the NKGB* and sent to the prison camps because he tried to stop the orgy of rape and murder in the border area. His crime: "Bourgeois Humanism".

The German authorities made full use of these atrocities for propaganda purposes. They still hoped to drive a wedge between the Soviet Union and their Anglo-American allies, and Nemmersdorf provided the right sort of evidence to support the Nazi argument that Germany was fighting for the survival of European civilisation against "barbarians from the East".

The propaganda failed to influence the Allies. But it succeeded too well among the German population. Panic set in throughout East Prussia. Hundreds of thousands of people fled from the homes they had lived in and the fields they had tilled for generations – which may, of course, have been precisely what Stalin intended when he turned his soldiers loose.

Long lines of carts and wheelbarrows and prams, piled high with precious possessions, headed west. On these

* Soviet security service, 1943-46. Renamed MGB in 1946; later became KGB.

Kopelev became friendly with Solzhenitsyn in the "Gulag Archipelago" and was the model for Rubin in *The First Circle*.

"treks", as they were called, besides Germans of the border area, there were prisoners of war of a dozen nationalities, including Russians who had no wish to explain to the NKGB how they had come to surrender, and refugees who had fled East to escape the bombing of their cities by the RAF and USAF. The lucky ones had farm tractors – until their fuel gave out. Some refugees disappeared in snow drifts, others were caught in crossfire, run over by tanks, or strafed by marauding Stormoviks, the ground attack aircraft which were feared by the Germans as *"Der Schwarze Tod"* (The Black Death). Yet on they plodded, a people on the march, looking for safety, doomed by their own leaders' excesses.

As the Russian armies drove towards Berlin, so the refugees were forced north, towards the sea. They headed for Elbing, the railway junction, Königsberg, the capital of East Prussia, and the ports of Danzig and Pillau. Some eventually got through to the West by train or truck convoy. But the majority concentrated in the Baltic ports, hoping to find ships to carry them to safety.

For a time, while Hossbach's men held the front, there was some organisation. Soup kitchens were set up. Pegs driven into the frozen shallows guided treks across the ice of the Frisches Haff, the sea lagoon which stretches from Königsberg to Elbing. For some, their luck and the ice held. But all too often the heavily-laden carts fell through, disappearing for ever.

Both Hossbach and General Guderian, the Panzer specialist who had been made Chief of Staff after the bomb plot against Hitler the previous July, had pleaded for the army to be allowed to evacuate their positions along the Latvian and Estonian coasts. They argued that the 300,000 men of Army Group North should be brought south to shield Berlin. But Hitler would have none of it. Now, the remnants of these armies were cut off. They had to be supplied by sea.

The last surviving pocket battleships and heavy cruisers of the German navy, the *Prinz Eugen*, *Lützow*, *Admiral Scheer*, and

Admiral Hipper, were formed into a task force, the 2nd Battle Group, and used to support the hard-pressed soldiers. Desperately, they turned the power of their big guns against the concentrations of Russian armour, artillery and men which were pushing the Germans back to the sea in shrinking pockets of blood and misery.

They could do little. The situation was hopeless and the soldiers knew it. Guderian toured the front and saw that the Russians were building up their forces for one final thrust into the heart of Germany. It was only a question of when the blow would fall.

It came on January 12th, 1945, with a two-hour artillery barrage which sent 117,000 shells crashing into the German line – much of it now held by old men and young lads armed with the hand-held Panzerfaust anti-tank weapon. On this frosty, clear day Marshal Rokossovsky's army thundered into East Prussia. The Russi.ns had ten times as many men as the Germans, seven times as many tanks and twenty times as many guns. The German front collapsed.

The Russians poured into the heartland of German militarism. Albert Speer, the Nazi Minister of War Production, tells in his book, *Inside the Third Reich*, of the remarkable scene which then ensued in Berlin.

We were standing around in the so-called Ambassador's Room at the Chancellery, a tapestried anteroom to Hitler's main office, waiting for the situation conference to begin. When Guderian arrived – he had been delayed by a call on the Japanese Ambassador Oshima – an orderly in a plain black-and-white SS uniform opened the door to Hitler's office. We walked across the heavy handwoven rug to the map table by the windows. The huge table top, a single slab of marble, had come from Austria; it was blood-red, striated with the beige and white cross-sections of an ancient coral reef. We took our positions on the window side; Hitler sat facing us.

The German army in Courland was hopelessly cut off. Guderian tried to convince Hitler that this position should be abandoned and the army transported across the Baltic Sea.

Hitler disagreed, as he always did when asked to authorise a retreat. Guderian did not give in. Hitler insisted, the tone sharpened, and finally Guderian opposed Hitler with an openness unprecedented in this circle. Probably fired by the drinks he had had at Oshima's, he threw aside all inhibitions. He stood facing Hitler across the marble table. Hitler too had risen to his feet.*

"It's simply our duty to save these people, and we still have time to remove them!" Guderian cried out in a challenging voice.

Infuriated, Hitler retorted: "You are going to fight on there. We cannot give up these areas!"

Guderian held firm: "But it's useless to sacrifice men in this senseless way," he shouted. "It's high time! We must evacuate those soldiers at once!"

. . . But Hitler stuck to his decision.

Hitler was aided in this madness by the Gauleiter of East Prussia, Erich Koch, a man who embodied all that was evil in Nazism. Koch, described by William Manchester as a "sour little martinet who habitually carried a stockwhip", had earlier held the post of Reich Commissar in the Ukraine, and there, in Kiev in 1943, he made a speech in which he said: "We are the Master Race and must govern hard but just . . . I will draw the very last out of this country. I did not come to spread bliss . . . The population must work, work, and work

* Oshima had tried repeatedly in 1942 and 1943 to persuade Hitler to make a separate peace with Russia so that the Germans and the Japanese could combine to defeat the United States and Great Britain. Hitler refused, according to Oshima, because Germany needed the Ukraine's wheat, which could only be wrested from them by force. But it is interesting to speculate on how much Oshima may have influenced Guderian in his desire to evacuate the East.

again . . . We definitely did not come here to give out manna. We have come here to create the basis for victory.

"We are a master race, which must remember that the lowliest German worker is racially and biologically a thousand times more valuable than the population here."

But now, Koch's days of strutting over a conquered race were gone. Instead, as a Reich Defence Commissar, he was struggling to maintain Hitler's writ inside East Prussia. His idea of defending the Reich was slavishly to follow Hitler's dictum that not one yard of German soil should be abandoned to the Russians.

Styling himself the Führer of the People's Army of East Prussia, he called on everyone to take up arms and refused to evacuate the civilian population except from a five-mile belt immediately behind the front line. He would not prepare for the evacuation of those outside this zone because "no true German would allow himself even the thought that East Prussia might fall into Russian hands". His so-called "People's Army" busied itself rounding up "cowards" and hanging them. He established his own arsenals and deprived the regular troops of badly-needed weapons and equipment. He spoke on the radio every night exhorting the people of East Prussia to continue the struggle. And when General Hossbach tried to fight his way out to the West, Koch sent a message to Hitler: "Fourth Army fleeing towards Reich, attempting cowardly breakthrough. I am carrying on the defence of East Prussia with the People's Army." Hitler countermanded the westward attack and Hossbach was sacked.

Yet all this time Koch had been preparing his own escape with his party cronies and his looted treasure. He had requisitioned two icebreakers, the *Ostpreussen* and the *Pregel*, and equipped them with special radio equipment and anti-aircraft guns.

This was the man into whose territories the refugees, panic-stricken by tales of what had happened at Nemmersdorf and other places, were now flooding. There were hundreds of thousands of them, fleeing just in front of the Russian T 34s as they swept aside the Volkssturm and their Panzerfausts. The regular German soldiers began to run as well, even those with medals for close-combat bravery who had fought all the way to Moscow and back, but now saw no point in dying for an already dead cause.

The excesses of the Russian soldiers grew worse the further they advanced into Germany. The dreaded order "*Frau Komm*" meant rape and probably death. The invaders spread syphilis wherever they went. They pillaged; and what they could not steal they smashed and burnt. Alexander Solzhenitsyn was there, serving in the Soviet artillery as a captain. He wrote later of his shame – shame for his comrades and himself – for he had succumbed and looted some fine writing paper and pencils and had gone to bed with a girl whose only plea was, "Don't shoot me".

He was arrested in East Prussia by the NKGB in early February partly because of his criticism of the officially-encouraged cruelties. In his monumental *Gulag Archipelago* he later recalled that "for three weeks the war had been going on inside Germany, and all of us knew very well that if the girls were German they could be raped and then shot".

While he was serving his sentence – eight years for "anti-Soviet propaganda" – in the severity of the Ekibastuz labour camp in northern Kazakhstan he composed an epic poem, *Prussian Nights*. He did not dare write it down but kept it in his head until his release. It tells of the terror that came to East Prussia:

> A moaning, by the walls half muffled:
> The mother's wounded, still alive.
> The little daughter's on the mattress,
> Dead. How many have been on it?
> A platoon, a company perhaps?
> A girl's been turned into a woman,
> A woman turned into a corpse.

It's all come down to simple phrases:
Do not forget! Do not forgive!
Blood for blood! A tooth for a tooth!
The mother begs, *"Töte mich, Soldat!"*

It must be re-emphasised that these atrocities were not simply the deeds of primitive soldiers from Siberia and Central Asia, maddened by battle. They were officially encouraged. Ilya Ehrenburg, the Russian war correspondent and propagandist, urged on the troops: "Kill. Kill. In the German race there is nothing but evil. Follow the precepts of Comrade Stalin.

"Stamp out the Fascist beast once and for all in its lair. Use force and break the racial pride of these Germanic women. Take them as your lawful booty. Kill. As you storm onwards, kill, you gallant soldiers of the Red Army."

There was criticism of Ehrenburg's wildness even in war-time Moscow, when *Pravda* published an article by Communist party theoretician G. F. Alexandrov in which he said it was un-Marxist and unwise to think that all Germans were Nazis, to be treated only as subhumans.

But the soldiers preferred to listen to Ehrenburg and to commanders like Colonel General Rybalko, whose daughter had been abducted by German soldiers and who, in consequence, had his own bitter payment to exact. Poised on the border of Germany, he whipped up his men: "The long-awaited hour, the hour of revenge is at hand! We all have personal reasons for revenge: my daughter, your sisters, our Mother Russia, the devastation of our land!"

Even the official Soviet *History of the Great Patriotic War of the Soviet Union*, while extolling the virtues of the Red Army, was forced to admit: "Not all Soviet troops correctly understood how they had to behave in Germany. In the first days of fighting in East Prussia there were some isolated acts of the violation of the correct norms of behaviour . . .". The fact that the Soviet historians, not noted for their ready admission of blame, were forced to record that the Red Army was not always correct indicates just how much "norms of behaviour" were violated.

But where could the Germans find safety? And how long could a stumbling column of refugees stay in front of the Russian tanks? For millions it seemed that the only hope of salvation lay in evacuation by the German Navy and Merchant Navy across the Baltic Sea. So they poured into the ports.

Scenes at the ports were horrific. Jürgen Thorwald in his *Flight Across the Sea* wrote:

Snow had been falling steadily for days. The streets were filled with deep snowdrifts. The wagons of the refugee treks, arriving in endless procession, looked like snowy hills. Refugees arrived in trains too; in wretched groups they flocked out of the station and ploughed through the streets to seek shelter in schools, barracks, or the port warehouses. They could be seen standing in long lines before the new navy relief stations and the soup kitchens that had been opened in the harbour sheds or makeshift wooden shelters.

Women muffled up to their eyes were going with their children from door to door, braving the wind and snow to beg for a bed or a cup of warm milk. There were children, too, who pulled their mothers along on sleighs or boards searching for a doctor, a bed, or just a warm corner . . .

The Countess zu Eulenberg told the authors what happened when the ship in which she was escaping from the small port of Neufahrwasser, just outside Danzig, called in to pick up yet more refugees at Pillau on the opposite side of the Bay of Danzig – closer to the Russians.

"As we arrived I looked out of the porthole and saw nothing but a thick ridge of snow. And when we came closer I realised this was a huge crowd of refugees waiting for a chance to get out. They had put up blankets like tents and had spent the night waiting. We came alongside and the gangway was put out. The crush to get on board was just terrible. I saw a pram being squeezed out of all recognition by the pushing masses. One old man fell into the water and there was nothing one could do in the crush – also it was so cold he would have died on hitting the water . . ."

As the Russians drew nearer, so the desperation increased. The Soviet guns hammered at the ports and the Stormoviks bombed and strafed, tearing great holes in the waiting ranks of refugees. But nobody moved, even death was less important than getting on board one of the boats. Babies were used as tickets, being carried on board and then thrown down again to be used as a passport to safety for another member of the family. Some fell between the ship and the quayside. It seemed not to matter. All that did matter was to get away from the Russians.

Even as late as January 30th, Hitler, in a speech over the radio, after referring to the "gruesome events which are taking place in the East", claimed that Germany would eventually triumph, and called for loyal obedience to order.

That same day his Deputy, Martin Bormann, wrote to his wife:

The Bolsheviks are ravaging everything. They regard rape as an everyday occurrence. You and the children must never fall into the hands of these wild beasts. But I hope very much that the danger will never arise, and that the Führer will succeed in parrying this blow, as he has parried others before it. Among the two or three millions who have been driven from hearth and home there is, as you may imagine, the most unutterable misery. The children are starving and freeze to death; and all we can do is harden our hearts and strive all the more fiercely to save the rest of our people, and to build up a new defence line. We must succeed.

25

Bormann, blind to the logic of revenge, was unable to accept the realities of the situation. One man who did accept them was Gross Admiral Karl Doenitz. Nine days previously, he had sent a one-word coded signal: HANNIBAL. It was the order for his submariners in the training depots at the now threatened port of Gdynia to flee to the West.

3

EVER SINCE HITLER had invaded Poland in 1939, Gdynia, re-named by Hitler himself as Gotenhafen or Goth's haven, had played a major part in the submarine campaign, launched by Admiral Raeder and carried on by Doenitz, to destroy Great Britain by cutting off the sea-borne supplies on which she depended.

The sheltered waters of the Bay of Danzig and the deeper sea off Bornholm were ideal for submarine training. In the early days of the war, crews trained there would join new boats at Kiel and Hamburg and sail across the North Sea and round the north of Scotland to join in the Battle of the Atlantic. Later, after the fall of France, they travelled over-land across Europe to sail on the boats based in the protected pens built at ports along the Bay of Biscay.

The submarine peril reached its peak in the spring of 1943. Then new detection and hunting techniques swung the war at sea in the Allies' favour, and it came to be assumed that the U-boats had been defeated.

But suddenly, in January 1945, the U-boats again became a menace. As Captain Stephen Roskill, the naval historian, has written:

> Surprising though it may seem, the early months of 1945 were an anxious period for the British naval authorities; for we knew that new U-boats were still taking to the water far faster than we were sinking them, we were expecting the greatly improved Type XXI and XXIII boats to enter service in some numbers, and we knew that since the arrival of the "Schnorkel" our radar fitted aircraft had lost much of their effectiveness.

Doenitz used the Schnorkel-fitted submarines in British coastal waters and they scored a number of successes. But although he was delighted with their performance, he was waiting impatiently for the new "electro-boats" which were far superior to everything previously built and would wipe out the technical superiority attained by the Allies' anti-submarine forces. Doenitz's ambitions were continually frustrated by bombing attacks which held up production, but he still hoped to get the new types of boat into action. And when that happened, he would need as crews the young men being trained in the Baltic ports.

For this reason, Doenitz was at first one of Hitler's main supporters in opposing a withdrawal that would mean imperilling or abandoning the Baltic ports. The new super U-boats represented his last gamble. But it was too late. By January 21st, the moment of decision had come.

The submarine training divisions were based in big merchant ships: the *Hansa*; the *Hamburg*; the *Deutschland*.

And the *Wilhelm Gustloff*.

4

THE *Wilhelm Gustloff*, in fact, had a special connection with the U-boat Service – and with the Nazi party. She was owned by the Deutsche Arbeitsfront, the German Labour Front, and before the war every one of her crew had to belong to the Nazi Party. A uniformed Nazi official, Group Leader Kaufhold, kept a vigilant eye on the Party's interests aboard, and when he was not engaged in his commissar-type duties he ran the ship's laundry.

The liner had her very origins in the Party, for Hitler had ordered her to be built and had then named her after Gauleiter Wilhelm Gustloff, leader of the German Nazis in Switzerland. In February 1936, Gustloff was assassinated by a young Yugoslav Jew, David Frankfurter, who obtained admission to his flat by pretending he had an urgent message, and then shot him five times in the head.

Gustloff had been a militant supporter of Hitler from the early days of the Nazi movement and his task in Switzerland had been to spread the Nazi doctrine among the German-Swiss and to collect information about anti-Nazi Germans living there. He was important enough for the consuls of a number of countries to be keeping an eye on his activities in Davos and for the Swiss government to ban his newspaper *Der Reichsdeutsche*. There were also demands that he should be expelled from Switzerland but they were blocked by Nazi sympathisers in the Swiss government. Until he was killed, few people in the outside world or, for that matter, in Germany itself, had heard of him. However, as the first Nazi assassinated by a Jew, he immediately became a martyr and an excuse for anti-semitic excesses.

His funeral rivalled that of the old President, Field Marshal von Hindenburg, in its display of official mourning. Hitler attended and, standing with Hess, Goebbels and Himmler, made a hysterical attack on the Jews:

"There marches before our eyes an endless line of murdered National Socialists, assassinated in cowardly fashion, almost always from behind, beaten down, stabbed or shot. Behind every murder is the same power which is responsible for this crime, the hate-inspired influence of our Jewish foes. We have done nothing to harm this enemy. Yet he attempted to place the German people beneath his yoke and make them his slaves. He is responsible for all the disasters Germany suffered in November 1918 and the years that followed . . . We hear the challenge and accept it . . . Dear comrades, you have not fallen in vain . . . The Jewish murderer never realised or foresaw that in killing one man, he aroused millions of comrades for all eternity to a true German life. Every section of the Party abroad now has its patron and sacred martyr to our ideal. His picture will hang in every office and he will never be forgotten.

"That is our oath. This deed falls back upon the doer. Germany will not thereby be weakened, but the power that was responsible for the crime . . ."

The Nazi newspaper *Völkische Beobachter* continued the agitation with an editorial which argued:

If the National Socialist attitude towards the Jews needed any justification, it is amply provided by this shameful act. Germany has already lost hundreds of her best citizens through the Jews. [This assertion was not explained.]

Murder is a weapon in the political struggle exclusively used by the Jews . . . This murder was made possible only by the atmosphere of hatred and envy of Germany created by the Jews

Gustloff's murder can therefore be seen as one of the early

steps on Hitler's road to the "Final Solution", his attempt to exterminate the Jews.*

Wilhelm Gustloff got his memorial on May 5th, 1937, when his widow, who had been very close to Hitler, launched the splendid liner which bore his name in Gothic letters on her bows. The new vessel had been built by Blohm and Voss at a cost of twenty-five million Reichsmarks as the flagship of the Strength Through Joy movement, run by the notorious drunkard Richard Ley, who got his joy through the strength of the liquor he consumed. The movement had been set up by Hitler to show the world how great were the achievements of his new Germany. It was a huge public relations exercise to demonstrate that German workers, happy in their labours, were able to enjoy every modern amenity.

In keeping with this ideal, the liner was a one-class ship which, with its crew of 400, was designed to take 1,465 happy passengers on holiday cruises to the Mediterranean and Africa as well as in the northern waters of Norway, where groups of Hitler Youth could revel in Nordic dreams.

She undertook her first cruise, to the Mediterranean, in March 1938 under the command of Captain Karl Lubbe. This was the era of the great transatlantic liners when British, French and American ships, with their luxuriously appointed first-class cabins for the rich, and far more spartan accommodation for the third-class travellers, were the living symbols of the class divisions of the capitalist world. So the *Wilhelm Gustloff* made a doctrinal point, that in Hitler's Germany it was the workers and the Nazi Party faithful who were treated like lords. As a German writer put it: "The *Gustloff* was not for the big and important people but for the locksmith from Bayreuth, the postman from Cologne, the cloakroom girl from Bremen, and the housewife."

With this background it was inevitable that her launching

---

* Frankfurter, ably defended by a Swiss lawyer who accused Gustloff of setting up a "miniature Gestapo" in Switzerland, was sentenced to eighteen years' imprisonment.

should be turned into a great propaganda exercise. Hitler was there with his entourage. There were bands and banners and a great cheering and blowing of sirens as she gathered speed down the slipway at Hamburg.

She succeeded admirably in fulfilling Hitler's intentions. She took workers to Italy for cruises costing only twelve pounds and in April 1938 she had a stroke of propaganda luck. Her radio officer picked up an SOS from the British collier *Pegaway*, in distress twenty miles off the Dutch island of Terschelling. She went to the rescue and saved nineteen members of the crew. Newspapers at the time were quick to make a point about the comradeship of the seas transcending political differences. Wherever she went she carried with her the aura of Germany's new-found power and efficiency. She cruised to Portugal and Madeira. On a visit to Britain she sailed up the Thames to be used as a floating polling station for 2,000 Germans wishing to vote in an election.

In the winter of 1938-39 she went to Genoa to pick up passengers who had travelled by rail from Germany and then sailed on to Naples and Palermo before putting her passengers ashore at Venice for their homeward rail journey. She made her last peacetime cruise in the early summer of 1939 to Norway and Sweden.

Then came the war and after only seventeen months of showing the flag she was taken into dock in Hamburg to be converted into a hospital ship. But she never served in that role, for in 1940 she sailed east to captured Gdynia to be used as barracks ship for the submariners at their training school. The richly decorated public rooms were filled with bunks for sailors who drilled on the sun deck, where lucky cruise passengers had tanned themselves in the Mediterranean heat. Her shining white paint was replaced with navy grey, her crack crew left to take part in the fighting and were replaced by Italian, Lithuanian and Croatian workers, whose job was to look after the submariners.

She lay alongside the pier at Gdynia for over four years and from her issued the stream of U-boat men who almost brought Britain to her knees. Admiral Doenitz, though he sent so many of them to their deaths – over ninety per cent of them perished – loved these men. He had become convinced that the U-boat arm represented all that was finest in the German fighting man.

And so, with the Russians heading inexorably for Gdynia, he decided to save the submariners. There was still a flicker of hope that they could man the new U-boats, but Doenitz's concern, in the last resort, was simply to save them from the Russians. It seemed only proper that the *Wilhelm Gustloff*, for so long their home, should be the ship ordered to carry them to safety.

5

WHILE DOENITZ WAS setting in motion Operation Hannibal, the Soviet Navy's Red Banner fleet of submarines, operating in the Baltic and the Gulf of Finland, was' poised to move over to the offensive.

The Red Army's advance westwards along the Gulf of Finland after lifting the siege of Leningrad, followed by the surrender of Germany's unfortunate ally, Finland, uncorked the Baltic for the submarines which had been bottled up for so long by mine barrages and anti-submarine nets in Leningrad and the fortress island of Kronstadt, the main Russian naval base in the Baltic.

Until the cork was pulled, the Red Banner fleet had a very thin time of it. When Hitler attacked, the Russian Navy operated a total of 218 submarines, the world's largest underwater fleet; and yet it achieved less than any of the other major submarine forces, sinking only 108 merchant ships and twenty-eight small warships for the loss of 108 submarines.

Stalin's pre-war purges had hit the submarine fleet hard. At the outbreak of war, only a quarter of its captains had more than two years' experience of command. And they had other problems. Their torpedoes were inefficient, exploding prematurely or not at all, and running wild. Their hydrophones, used for listening to enemy ships, were crude in comparison with those of both the British and the Germans. Their submarines had noisy engines, which gave their own position away. And their crews were depleted by having technicians withdrawn to serve with the Red Army.

Stalin had shown little interest in the navy in the early years of the war, but in December 1944 he discussed the Baltic with Admiral Nikolai Kuznetsov, a survivor of the purges who had risen in less than three years from captain of a cruiser to Commander in Chief of the Soviet naval forces.

Kuznetsov later told friends what happened when the Russian dictator summoned him. Stalin told the Admiral that it was time the Baltflot showed what it could do. It must play a full part in the offensive by attacking German sea communications and protecting its own waters against the German U-boats and surface ships, for German pocket battleships and cruisers were still patrolling the Baltic coasts, using their heavy guns against the advancing Russians.

Not only, said Stalin, did he expect a significant increase in the success rate of the Baltic submarine flotilla but he wanted more use made of the surface vessels. The Air Force would be ordered to retain air supremacy, and would improve long-range reconnaissance in order to help the fleet.

The truth of the matter is that the heavy ships of the Russian Navy did not dare venture out. Mostly obsolescent, unused for four years except as support artillery, with many sailors drafted to fight as infantry ashore, they would have been no match for battle-hardened ships such as the *Admiral Hipper*.

Kuznetsov apparently displayed a great deal of courage in pointing out the realities of the situation to Stalin, explaining about the mines which still littered the Gulf of Finland, the icy conditions which hampered movement and the lack of training imposed by the long siege of Leningrad.

Stalin dismissed him, saying: "I have given you a submarine fleet second to none. Now use it to its full potential."

It was a statement which was far from accurate but it brooked no argument; so the submarines, operating from Finnish ports kept open by icebreakers, were given orders to go out and sink whatever they saw. The aim of their operation was both military and psychological. They were to attack the convoys taking supplies in to the beleaguered German Army and carrying refugees and soldiers out to safety; and in so doing they would exact a terrible revenge for the losses

35

and humiliations they had suffered in the past four years.

This was the mission that took Captain Third Class Sasha Marinesko and the Russian submarine S 13 to their meeting with the *Wilhelm Gustloff*.

6

MARINESKO HAD BEEN born in Odessa, on the Black Sea, of a Ukrainian mother and a Rumanian father who had served in the Rumanian Navy and had fled from Constanzia after being sentenced to death for taking part in one of the many mutinies that broke out during the Balkan Wars.

One of the young Marinesko's early memories was of running down to the shore on a February day in 1920, when he was seven years old, to watch the "Interventionists" and "Whites" flee from Odessa. The port had changed hands several times during the civil war which followed the Bolshevik Revolution in 1917 and at one time it had been occupied by British and French troops.

Before the First World War Odessa was one of the most beautiful cities in Tsarist Russia as well as being a thriving port and industrial centre. More like a French cathedral city than a dreary Russian provincial town, it had seafront palaces for the aristocracy, broad boulevards lined with acacias, neat squares, an elegant university and splendid mansions for the merchants.

But Marinesko's father, who had changed his name from the Rumanian Marinescu, lived in the poor area of low-lying docklands, wharves and ship repair yards. His neighbours were Russians, Ukrainians, Armenians, Moldavians, Turks, Greeks, Bulgarians, gypsies and Jews. But they all referred to their city as "Mother Odessa" and they were flattered to be called Odessans.

Civil war and Soviet rule swept away the elegance and private prosperity of Odessa. The port, blockaded by the "Interventionists", was deserted, its inhabitants now mostly huge ginger wharf-rats and hungry cats. There was little to eat or drink and the city shrank to 100,000 people who were prepared to try their luck with the Bolsheviks.

Growing up during the city's years of turmoil, Marinesko hunted with fierce gangs of urchins, fighting for scraps of food and mixing with thieves, forgers, fences and racketeers. Playing truant from school, he worked as a human scarecrow, keeping sparrows off the vegetable patches established on disused piers, and he fished for bullheads and mackerel in the silent harbour.

The first money he saw, and may even have stolen, was a "lemon", a yellow Soviet million rouble note – such was the inflation following the flight of the White Army. He stole anything he could lay his hands on, especially newspapers and wood for fuel, and hunted in the bazaar which had become a refuge for "Blatnye", the companionship of thieves.

When the troubles ended and Odessa settled down to its new way of life under Communism, the cargo and passenger ships with their strange foreign flags and coloured funnels once again sailed past the Vorontsov lighthouse into port and Marinesko found a new way of making money; diving for coins tossed into the sea by passengers on the cruise liners.

Even the dull dangers of Soviet rule did not destroy Odessa's reputation for diversity, gaiety and cunning, nor eradicate the Odessans' traditional wit and irreverence. Marinesko was brought up on its special kind of jokes, songs, stories and curses. His rule of life was one he learned in the bazaar and often quoted: "If you want to eat, know how to sell the sleeves of a waistcoat."

He left school at the age of fifteen in 1928, having been taught to read and write and not much else. Like a true Odessan he spoke a strange dialect with Latin roots, Slav prefixes, and a few Yiddish suffixes. He misplaced the accent when he spoke Russian, his grammar was never perfected and his verbs were often wrongly conjugated. He was already a "character" in speech and style.

He got a job as a cabin boy on a cargo ship. But an official with an eye for a likely lad spotted him and within a year he was given a place at the Odessa Naval Institute. He progressed to become a mate on a coaster, the *Black Sea*, which plied from Odessa along the small ports to Batumi in the south.

The breakthrough in his career came when, off Skadovsk, he acted bravely and decisively to save the crew of a torpedo boat which capsized in a storm. News of the incident spread through the Black Sea Fleet and in 1935 he was ordered to transfer to the Navy and join a navigator's course. A year later he switched to submarines and found his true métier.

He was a natural for submarines. His urchin upbringing had made him resourceful, capable of coping with emergencies calmly, and he discovered the gift of leadership. He also saw that in the Navy he would be a nonentity unless he opted for the small ships where there would be scope for his individualism. He chose to go into submarines at exactly the right time. Crews were needed for the new boats then being built. The training was intense and rigorous. He gloried in it, became a member of Komsomol, the Young Communist organisation, and joined in the worship of Stalin. He did not, however, neglect the vodka and the girls.

After nine months' training he was appointed navigator of the Shch 306, otherwise known as the *Piksha* (Haddock) which had been commissioned a year before. Six months later he was sent back to school to take a commander's course, and then, in the summer of 1937, was appointed to command the submarine M 96.

That was the time when the Soviet Navy was being torn apart by the purges. Marinesko kept his head down and concentrated on making his boat the best in the fleet.

Launched shortly before he took command, the submarine was an improvement on the earlier M-class, useful only in coastal waters. It displaced only 250 tons, and was just forty-five metres long. It could reach fourteen knots on the surface, cruise at three knots submerged, and dive to a maximum depth of eighty metres. There were eighteen crew. It was cramped, had only one 45 mm gun and two torpedo tubes, but it was ideal as a first command for a cocky young officer.

In the naval archives at Gatchina, forty-eight kilometres south of Leningrad, there is a file on the M 96 in which it is recorded that for two years the vessel was designated the best-trained and most efficient submarine in the Baltic Fleet. It established a diving record of nineteen and a half seconds compared with the average time in the fleet of twenty-eight seconds. And in 1940 Marinesko and his torpedomen were given gold watches for their marksmanship. They were now ready for war.

For most of the war, Marinesko suffered the frustrations common to all Russian submarine commanders in the Baltic, and there are conflicting reports about precisely what successes he achieved.

One Soviet writer, Captain Vladimir Dmitriyev, in his book *Submarines Attack*, reports that in 1942 the M 96 under Marinesko's command sank a 7,000-ton transport, and subsequently escaped twenty depth charges dropped by submarine chasers. But the official Soviet records for the period credit Marinesko with the sinking of only a 1,850-ton vessel.

By 1944, Marinesko was in charge of a larger submarine, the S 13. This was in fact a German designed boat, the product of secret arrangements made by Stalin and Hitler before the war. Marinesko was lucky to have left the *Piksha* and the M 96, both of which were later mined and lost with all hands.*

* The S 13 was a Stalinets class boat designed in 1933 at the Hague office of "Ingeniers-Kantoor voor Scheepsbouw" a company which was owned jointly by the German Navy, Krupps Germania-Werft of Kiel and the Deutsche Schiff und Maschinenbau AG of Bremen. The company was run by a retired German naval captain called Blum and had a staff of thirty. It had been set up in Holland specifically to evade the restrictive clauses of the Treaty of Versailles and the Stalinets submarines were a prime example of the illegal industrial-military cooperation between Germany and Russia before the war.

In this boat he sank a vessel on the Stolpe Bank, off Pomerania. The German naval historian, Professor Rohwer, dismisses the sinking as "insignificant", saying that the victim was a 563-ton trawler, the *Siegfried*. Russian sources, however, say that the *Siegfried* was a 5,000-ton cargo ship. The Russian account says that Marinesko fired three torpedoes from periscope depth at a range of 1,000 metres. All missed when the *Siegfried*'s captain took evasive action.

According to his crew, Marinesko was furious. He fired again, and again missed. Unable to re-load, he surfaced and shelled the *Siegfried* with his 100 mm gun. The cargo vessel returned machine-gun fire as shells crashed into her. Eventually, repeated hits from the submarine demolished her bridge and sank her.

Whatever the truth about these exploits, it is a fact that Marinesko enjoyed being treated as a hero for sinking two German ships. And in truth he was the very stuff of which Soviet heroes are made – a "new Soviet man". He was decisive, dedicated and had that rare gift of leadership which enabled him to switch from being Comrade Captain to Comrade messmate without losing authority. He was also a member of the Communist Party, which was an honour in itself, not granted to all, and he wore the medals of the Order of Lenin and the Order of the Red Banner on his tunic. These fell short of the highest award, "Hero of the Soviet Union", but were nevertheless substantial commendations.

At the end of 1944, the S 13 lay at the docks in the "Smolny" base in Turku, Finland's oldest city, by then under Soviet jurisdiction. The boat had been provisioned and fuelled. Stalin's orders to strike in the Baltic had been received at the base and the boat was due to sail on January 2nd to be on station in time for the new offensive designed to sweep the Germans from the Baltic states and East Prussia.

The submarine and her crew were ready. Unfortunately Marinesko was not.

He had been on a monumental bender which had lasted

three days and, as he dimly remembered later, took in huge quantities of *pontikka*, a spirit distilled from potatoes which made vodka seem like mother's milk. He had also enjoyed the favours of a number of women; just how many and in which particular establishment he couldn't remember.

He did not return to his boat. The naval patrols began looking for him. It was not until January 3rd, after being dried out in a sauna, that he returned to the base. He was in deep trouble, for Soviet officers are not in the habit of disappearing while ashore in foreign countries, especially during wartime and in a country which had been enemy territory a few months before. The authorities get anxious: they fear the comrade has defected or become a spy. That escapade in Turku was eventually to have cruel and calamitous consequences for Marinesko's career.

At first it seemed that he would get away with a rap over the knuckles from his forty-three-year-old commanding officer, Captain First Rank Alexander Yevstafyevitch Oryel, a pre-war submariner who took every opportunity to go to sea with his boats. He was widely regarded as being a fair and sensible commander, who ensured that as far as possible political considerations did not interfere with practical training.

Oryel understood Marinesko, and listened patiently to whatever the hungover skipper could remember of the lost three days. He was sure that there was no treachery behind Marinesko's behaviour; that it was an old-fashioned Russian carouse. And, as he needed all the good men he could find to carry out Stalin's command to "use the submarine fleet to its full potential", he decided to reprimand his wayward ace and get the S 13 to sea as quickly as possible.

But he had reckoned without the NKGB and the Deputy Commander for Political Affairs, Captain Jumkochiyan. They put Marinesko through a rigorous interrogation at the end of which Jumkochiyan recommended that he should be court martialled or, at least, returned to Kronstadt under escort.

It is not surprising that the watchdogs were suspicious. The

42

Russian Navy has something of a reputation for challenging political authority, both that of the Tsars and of the Kremlin. It was the cruiser *Aurore* which fired the first shot in the October Revolution and it was the sailors at Kronstadt who staged the first revolt against Communism. So the secret policemen hammered away at Marinesko, trying to force a confession out of him. He insisted he could not remember the name of the girls he had made love to or where their brothel was. But he confessed to everything else – leaving the base without permission, getting drunk, fraternising with the Finns, failing to report for duty.

He really had no option. His proclivities were well known and he agreed readily that he had committed these familiar sins of matelots on a "run ashore". But he became enraged when secret police accused him of treachery. There was a mutual loss of temper and Jumkochiyan read him a lecture on patriotism and the responsibilities that go with membership of the Communist Party.

Faced with Jumkochiyan's demands for a court martial, Captain Oryel avoided making an immediate decision. He had sent a report to the submarine brigade commander, Captain Verkhovsky, and insisted that he would not be hurried into a course of action which would affect the striking power of his division. Moreover, he flatly refused to accept that Marinesko had been recruited by the Nazi, British, American, Finnish or any other intelligence organisation.

It was the officers and crew of the S 13, led by Marinesko's friend and second in command, Lev Yefremenkov, now a Captain Lieutenant and member of the Order of the Red Banner, who forced the issue. After a meeting on board the submarine which for the secret police had disturbing echoes of the Kronstadt Mutiny of 1921, they presented a petition to Oryel demanding that their commander be allowed to rejoin the vessel. The petition was drafted largely by Yefremenkov and was unanimously approved. It pointed out that the "Fascists are not yet beaten", and in the grandiose patriotic language which was fashionable in Russia at the time declared: "Motherland, hear us! We swear to you that we will take terrible revenge for the blood, suffering, grief and tears of our fathers, mothers and children. We swear that ceaselessly, day and night, we will seek out and sink enemy ships. We swear to uphold and extend the sacred military traditions of the Baltic sailors."

All very well, but by their action the crew of the S 13 were inviting trouble. Captain Oryel could not believe that the incident was going to develop into a mutiny on one of the best submarines in the Fleet. But he feared that the "Ukrainian boys" who effectively ran the boat would do something foolish if Marinesko was court martialled. A rough, tough group of men, they could be as reckless as their commander. And he knew that if there was trouble on the S 13 and the crew refused to sail without their captain, the NKGB would deal with it swiftly and brutally. Moreover, he, too, would certainly be court martialled for allowing the affair to get out of hand.

He called in Marinesko and Yefremenkov and gave them their orders to put to sea. But while he could get them out of the tense atmosphere of Turku and the clutches of Jumkochiyan, he could not risk allowing them to regard the affair as finally closed. He ordered them to sail in the S 13 east to Hangö where they were to wait until January 11th, by which time he would have heard from Kronstadt if Marinesko was to be court martialled or not. If all went well, they were to take the S 13 down to the Bay of Danzig and cause trouble for the Germans there, and not for him in Turku.

Rear Admiral Nikolai Smirnov, member of the Military Council of the Baltic Fleet, recalled in his memoirs that when reports of the incident reached him, he flew to Helsinki from Leningrad to find out what was going on. He wrote:

Some of our political officers warned us that there had been unpleasant events and that we had to be especially vigilant.

44

The enemy were still active and were attempting to subvert our forces . . . I was impressed with the spirit and determination of our submariners to take the fight to the enemy. No one wanted to remain in harbour. In any case, conditions would not allow it. The enemy had to be beaten.

So Marinesko, for the time being, was off the hook. But there is no doubt that if it had not been for Stalin's order for the submarines to launch all-out warfare on the German supply routes and the consequent necessity to have every submarine at sea, Marinesko, instead of conning his boat out of Hangö harbour on January 11th, would have been on his way to Siberia – or worse.

Already he was a marked man. The NKGB attached to naval headquarters at Kronstadt had lost no time in opening a file on Captain Third Class Alexander Marinesko, Order of Lenin, Order of the Red Banner. War hero or not, he was on their list. Because of his crew, Oryel, and the need for submarine captains he would be late arriving in the Gulag Archipelago. But, in due course, he would get there.

7

MARINESKO SLIPPED OUT of Hangö early on January 11th. With an icebreaker opening up the route for her, the S 13 was on her way back to the war. One of the fleet's best navigators, Captain Lieutenant Nikolai Redkoborodov, a twenty-four-year-old Leningrader, had joined the crew, and the submarine was laden with twelve torpedoes, 120 rounds of ammunition for its 100 mm gun and a quantity of anti-aircraft ammunition. She was provisioned for a long patrol and, although we have no direct knowledge of Marinesko's thoughts as he set out, it is certain that he was determined to make it a success. For now, in addition to the normal reasons, he needed to wipe away the stain of his escapade at Turku. The crew would also have wanted a success to balance their act of near-mutiny. As they turned south-west to zig-zag down into the Baltic, past the west coast of Gotland Island, it can be assumed that they were a determined group and, in their captain's case, possibly desperate for some redeeming triumph.

But nothing came their way. The Baltic was empty of the rich prizes they expected and needed, and, when the S 13 surfaced nine days later at a point well south of Gotland to re-charge her batteries and report to base, Marinesko had nothing to give except the simplest information about his position, course, fuel stocks and weather conditions. He was frugal to the point of meanness with his signals to head-quarters. He was never happy when the wireless mast was raised because he was sure that he could be "fixed" by German direction-finding stations operating along the coast. He believed that indiscreet wireless traffic was more to blame for the high rate of Soviet submarine casualties than any other cause – just as it had been responsible for a large proportion of U-boat casualties during the early days of the Battle of the Atlantic.

Therefore the cumbersome but usually reliable Bukhta set on the S 13 was used as little as possible, giving Petty Officer Telegraphist Mikhail Kolodnikov more time to perform his other task of controlling the food supplies. But on this occasion he had to keep the set open because there was a longish reply following the usual acknowledgment. Yefremenkov decoded it and passed it to Marinesko. It said: "From HQ Baltic Fleet to all submarines: Red Army offensive targeted on Danzig going well and likely to force enemy to evacuate Königsberg soon. Expect significant increase in movement of enemy transports in the region of the Danzig Bay."

Cheering news, but still the S 13 found no worthwhile target. The boat slipped into the routine of a long patrol, lying submerged during the day and surfacing at night to recharge the batteries and let out the stench of forty-six men crowded into a steel cigar. Then came orders to join a "wolf-pack" gathering off Memel, the Hanseatic port that had been cut off but was still being stubbornly defended by men of Hossbach's Fourth Army. It was about to be assaulted by General Bagramyan's 1st Baltic Front and the submarines were to attack any ships attempting to support them or to bring them out.

Shortly after dawn on January 26th, the S 13 joined two other submarines, the Shch 310 and the Shch 307, a few kilometres off the port. Marinesko had been given a fixed ten kilometre patrol line running parallel with the coast.

The Shch 307, named the *Treska* (Cod) and commanded by Captain Lieutenant Mikhail Kalinin, was to the north-east. The *Cod* was one of the most successful Soviet submarines, having been credited with sinking the U-boat U 144 and three ships each of about 3,000 tons. It survived the war and its conning tower has been set up as a memorial to submariners at the Kronstadt training school.

The Shch 310, named the *Byelukha* (White Whale), was at

the northern point of the ambush. Its commander was Captain Third Rank S. H. Bogorad, another experienced submariner who claimed to have sunk four ships, one of nearly 5,000 tons, in the eastern Baltic during a patrol the previous November when the *White Whale* was the first of the Soviet submarines to break out of the Gulf of Finland.

One of the objections to accepting these claims for successes is that throughout the war the Soviet High Command consistently and deliberately claimed far more ships sunk than was actually the case. This is fair in wartime as a means of confusing and demoralising the enemy, but normally when hostilities are over the correct figures are given, as, for instance, the RAF has correctly given the number of German aircraft shot down in the Battle of Britain. The Soviets, however, still cannot bring themselves to do this and they persist with their wartime fantasies – perhaps partly to ward off criticism that the Russian Navy did little to help the British-American convoys which suffered such terrible losses running supplies to Murmansk for the Russian armies. A good case in point is probably the battleship *Tirpitz*. The Russians still claim that the *Tirpitz* was hit by two torpedoes from the K 21 in the Barents Sea in July 1942. German records show that not only was the *Tirpitz* not hit but also that no torpedo tracks were sighted. It is thus ironic that when eventually Marinesko scored the greatest ever success of the Russian submarine fleet the very people who put out fictitious success stories stubbornly refused to believe him.

However, off Memel in those last few days of January 1945 there was nothing for any of the waiting submarines and when, before dawn on January 30th, Marinesko received a signal to the effect that the Red Army had occupied the port and resistance had ended, it became obvious that nothing would come.

Marinesko called a conference of his officers to discuss the situation. They had plenty of fuel left, enough food for another couple of weeks, and all their torpedoes.

How should they use them? It seemed obvious that the Bay of Danzig had to be the centre of German operations. In its sheltered waters the many small harbours and the major ports of Gdynia and Pillau offered sanctuary for the fleeing Germans and their convoys. Marinesko decided to leave the patrol line to which the S 13 had been ordered and head for the hunting grounds which he was sure would be full of quarry. He had made the correct assessment of the military situation. But unfortunately he neglected to tell his head-quarters what he planned and so when he swung the S 13 round on course for a point just north of the Hela Peninsula, the thin finger of land poking into the north-west corner of the Bay of Danzig, the Russian naval headquarters at Kronstadt had no idea where he was going or what he was planning.

8

Wʜɪʟᴇ ᴛʜᴇ S 13 was sailing south, there was frantic activity at Gdynia to speed the evacuation of refugees, wounded soldiers, and Doenitz's submarine specialists. Much of that activity centred round the *Wilhelm Gustloff*.

She was, of course, no longer the elegant cruise ship which had sailed the sunny Mediterranean in peacetime. Many of her lifeboats had been removed during her long period of immobility. The swimming pool had been drained to provide living accommodation.

And she was under a strange dual command. Her master was Captain Friedrich Petersen, a worn-out sixty-seven-year-old Merchant Navy officer who had been a prisoner of war, but had been repatriated by the British who considered that he could not possibly be of any further use to the German war effort. But as Military Commander, supervising her role as a submarine base ship, she had a regular Navy officer, Commander Wilhelm Zahn, a temperamental submariner.

Zahn lived on the ship, and was a well-known figure, partly because he always had with him his big Alsatian dog, Hassan. He was a fussily efficient disciplinarian, conscious of his position as senior naval officer aboard. His career had not quite lived up to his expectations. One incident, in particular, rankled. In 1939 he claimed to have hit the battleship *Nelson* with three torpedoes – but none exploded. Curiously, the Royal Navy's records – meticulously kept in regard to submarine attacks – do not record the incident.

What no doubt compounded Zahn's disappointment was the mistaken German belief that Winston Churchill was on board the *Nelson*. Doenitz records that he (Zahn) was so depressed by this failure, in which he was in no way to blame, that he felt compelled to withdraw him for the time being from active operations and employ him as an instructor at home.

Although he later returned to sea and scored some minor successes, he never seemed to find another opportunity for greatness. By the early summer of 1942 he was transferred permanently to the training division at Gdynia, a somewhat disappointed professional officer.

Now he summoned the leading officers of the *Wilhelm Gustloff* to a conference in the wardroom. Among those present were the white-haired Captain Petersen; his first officer and old friend, Louis Reese; Gerhardt Luth, the Purser; and Franz Lobel, the Chief Engineer.

According to Heinz Schoen, a trainee purser on board at the time who has since built up a *Gustloff* library of memories, Zahn called the meeting to order and told them: "Gentlemen, I have brought you here to deliver an order which affects both the Training Division and the *Wilhelm Gustloff*." He then explained the Doenitz order at some length and stressed the importance of speed in preparing for sea.

The ship was to be ready to sail within forty-eight hours. Many of the 2,000 naval personnel on board were to go ashore to help defend the port until the evacuation was complete. The next task would be to embark seriously wounded soldiers who had arrived in Gdynia aboard a hospital train from the East. Then refugees were to be taken on board.

From the purely Service point of view, by far the most important section of the *Wilhelm Gustloff*'s human cargo would be the 1,500 men of the submarine service, along with many of their dependants. But they would be only a small proportion of those who would sail in the former cruise ship. Every available corner would be packed with refugees.

"This will be no Strength Through Joy cruise," warned Zahn, according to Schoen. "All of us, both Navy and Merchant Navy officers, have a difficult task and bear heavy responsiblity. It is our duty to do everything possible to make things easier for the refugees and I expect the crew to go out of their way to be helpful."

The officers had known each other for a long time and Zahn did not feel it necessary to give detailed orders about what needed to be done. Although a great deal of hard work awaited them, the officers and crew were delighted at the thought that they would soon be at sea again, steaming West, away from the Red Army.

The build-up for the German Dunkirk had been rapid, spectacular, and efficient. Doenitz himself had taken over control of all the merchant ships that could be gathered together for the evacuation. They had previously been controlled by Herr Kaufman, the Gauleiter of Hamburg, who was also the Reich Commissioner for Shipping, but Doenitz took over to ensure smoother cooperation with the Navy. He appointed Rear Admiral Konrad Engelhardt, a man with considerable experience of the Merchant Navy, to coordinate the work of the two services. Admiral Kummetz, of Naval High Command East operating out of Kiel, was given control of the Western Baltic and Admiral Burchardi, a hard-liner given to making "fight to the last man" speeches, was put in charge of the Eastern Baltic and the Prussian coast.

Ships of all sorts, shapes and sizes were assembled, among them the big ships which had once been the pride of the German shipping lines, the *Hansa*, 23,130 tons, the *Hamburg*, 22,117 tons, the *Deutschland*, 21,046 tons, the *Cap Arkona*, 27,561 tons, the *Wilhelm Gustloff*, and eight other liners of over 10,000 tons, all of them employed as accommodation and mother ships for the submarine training divisions. Another 25 substantial cargo ships were ordered to join in the evacuation.

The *Hansa* was earmarked to carry the equipment of the training divisions, the officers and 3,000 refugees. The *Wilhelm Gustloff* was ordered to embark the 2nd Training Division, a contingent of women auxiliaries and a number of badly wounded soldiers.

The remainder of the naval personnel were to go aboard the

Hamburg and the *Deutschland*. In addition, they were instructed to make all additional space available to civilian refugees.

By the evening of January 22nd the crew of the *Gustloff* was hard at work preparing the ship to receive thousands of passengers, many of them wounded, all of them cold and exhausted. That side of the task presented no insuperable difficulties, because the liner had been run as a floating hotel for several years. But there were other problems. The ship had not sailed for four years; she had suffered some bomb damage and as the Chief Engineer worked among his artificers in the engine room he knew she would never be able to manage her old top speed of sixteen knots.

Walter Knust, the *Gustloff*'s second engineer, was on good terms with Commander Zahn. In quieter times they used to have a swim together in the ship's pool (since then drained to provide living accommodation) and then drink a leisurely glass of champagne. The Commander said to him, "Now we've got our sailing orders", and from that moment the engineers worked ceaselessly to make the *Gustloff* ready for sea. In the words of Knust: "For the next forty-eight hours we never even had five minutes off for a smoke."

First the *Gustloff* had to be fuelled. During the long period that she had been lying at the pier she had needed neither oil nor coal, because steam for heating had been piped aboard from a shore station and the harbour power station supplied her with electricity. Fuelling took some time and then Herr Knust and the Chief Engineer had to get up steam to test the boilers before releasing it and starting all over again.

On the bridge the atmosphere was by no means entirely cordial. Both Captain Petersen and First Officer Reese were executives without recent sea time. Reese, like Petersen, had fallen into British hands at the beginning of the war and like him had only been repatriated through the Red Cross because the British authorities felt that he was no longer fit for service. As part of the deal for his own repatriation, Petersen had signed an undertaking that he would not go to sea again as

53

ship's master. He had been the Liegerkapitan (sleeping captain) of a dockbound ship.

To stiffen the command, two young Merchant Navy officers, Captain Kohler and Captain Weller, were sent to join the *Wilhelm Gustloff* as senior officers of the watch. When they arrived at midday on January 27th there were thousands of people on the quay. There were sentries on the ship's gangway, soldiers with guns and steel helmets who checked everybody's papers. The arrival of the two captains brought forth a remark from one of the soldiers that they would soon be on their way. But it did not solve the problem of command that had arisen, for there was a serious split between the civil and military officers on board.

In normal circumstances a "sleeping captain" such as Petersen would never have been asked to take the liner to sea. But there was a grave shortage of ships' masters and he did have the advantage of having commanded the *Wilhelm Gustloff* before, on one of her peacetime voyages. He therefore assumed that in the traditional language of the sea he would be "sole master aboard, under God, for this voyage".

But the authorities, in the chaos that prevailed at that time, had been unable to come to any decision about the status of the ship. Already the command structure was sagging under the pressure of war and the proximity of the Russians. No ruling was given on whether the *Wilhelm Gustloff* was to be considered a naval troopship, a refugee liner, or a hospital ship. In truth she was a bit of each. Many people in Germany today believe that she was marked with the red crosses which identify a hospital ship but if this was so it was a breach of the Geneva Convention, for she was a ship of the German Navy and was armed with anti-aircraft guns.

9

ZAHN, THE SENIOR naval officer on board the *Wilhelm Gustloff*, did not like taking orders from a civilian even though Petersen was a Merchant Navy officer and nominally in charge of the ship. For the time being Zahn busied himself with military duties, seeing to the preparation of anti-aircraft positions. He also checked the signals equipment and the emergency stores. He had no written instructions, for the authorities had no time for such niceties. And there was nothing laid down which said that as a naval officer he had authority over the Merchant Navy officers. As he said later: "Naturally it is difficult to give orders to a sixty-seven-year-old captain trained to take complete responsibility for his ship during fifty years' experience at sea unless higher authority has been given."

Even so, he thought that Petersen was out of touch with modern warfare and was not capable of commanding the *Wilhelm Gustloff* at sea. From the start there was friction between the ageing Merchant Navy officers and the submarine officers who considered themselves the élite of the armed forces. It was an uncomfortable atmosphere that confronted the two thirty-five-year-olds, Kohler and Weller.

Another difficulty which faced them was that over the years that the ship had been lying at the quayside, her sea-going crew had been run down to a minimum. There were plenty of stewards to look after the submarine officers who lived on board, but few sailors. Many had been sent away to more active sea duties. Others had been drafted into the Naval Infantry Brigades raised to help support the army, now so short of manpower. By the time the ship was ordered to sea again, at least a third of the remaining deckhands were Croatians and other non-Germans.

Zahn, as a submariner, knew the dangers that the ship would run with such a crew and with a worn-out captain, and so he made several visits to operational headquarters to study the reports of hostile submarine activity in the Baltic. On each occasion he was told that the Navy had no firm reports of Soviet U-boats operating in the area through which the ship would sail. The Russian submarines had had so little success in the Baltic that while it was known that some had made the passage through the Gulf of Finland, they were thought to be few and badly handled and were not considered a menace. Soviet torpedo planes and the RAF's Bomber Command with its big bombs and mines were thought to represent a greater threat. But even they were considered no danger to the *Wilhelm Gustloff*. Her size and speed, her prestige as both a Nazi and submarine service flagship, somehow seemed to guarantee invulnerability. Obviously she would get through . . .

Stab Führerin Wilhelmina Reitsch, who was in Gdynia in command of 10,000 Women Naval Auxiliaries, told the authors: "We considered the *Wilhelm Gustloff* a safe and comfortable ship. It was for that reason that it became the first official evacuation ship for our girls." Frau Reitsch, who now lives in Hamburg, is the wife of Captain Karl Reitsch, a close friend of Admiral Doenitz and brother of the renowned test pilot, Hanna Reitsch. It was Hanna who flew into Berlin with Luftwaffe General von Greim – who was wounded during the flight – just a few days before Hitler's suicide, landing her plane on the road at the Brandenburg Gate under shellfire, in a vain mission to persuade Hitler to save himself.

"We decided that the girls had to be saved from the Russians," said Wilhelmina Reitsch, "and because road and rail transport was so dangerous at the time, it was considered best to send these girls, all aged between seventeen and twenty-five, on the *Gustloff*. The number of places available was limited so we carefully sifted through the auxiliaries and gave seaborne evacuation priority to those who had family or other responsibilities."

The navy girls greeted the news that they were to be taken westwards aboard ship with enthusiasm. For weeks they had heard reports of rape and murder as the Soviet Army battered its way into Prussia, and they had been told by refugees that it would be better to die than fall into the hands of the Russians.

They also dreaded the prospect of a long and perilous journey by train or truck convoy which might easily be intercepted by the advancing enemy. The bitter cold of the winter was yet another enemy to be feared – towards the end of January, the thermometer was registering twenty degrees below zero. For the girls a journey across the Baltic in a big liner seemed much more comfortable as well as safe.

In principle they were correct. As Admiral Doenitz points out: "Ninety-nine per cent of the refugees brought out by sea succeeded in arriving safely at ports on the western Baltic. The percentage of refugees lost on the overland route was very much higher."

But there was one girl who did not relish sailing on the liner. According to Schoen, a twenty-year-old from Hagen named Anni Faust had a premonition of disaster. While her friends were still celebrating the good news, she tried to give up her place: "I won't go on that death ship. I don't want to go on the *Gustloff*." But she had no choice. With the rest of the 373 Auxiliaries in their smart blue-grey uniforms of knee-length skirts and tunics, and wearing their forage caps with the eagle and swastika badge, she was embarked on the liner.

Most of the girls were settled down on E Deck in the drained swimming pool so that their officers could keep an eye on them. There were girls from all walks of life. Some were fresh from school, but others had worked in bars, theatres and other, more dubious places of entertainment in the Baltic ports. "They were quite a handful at the best of times," said one of their officers.

She recalled that about 500 of the girls were originally

selected. The ship's papers show that 373 embarked on the *Wilhelm Gustloff*. Some army girls were also put on board along with the wives and families of the permanent staff of the submarine training school. These last had priority since the *Wilhelm Gustloff* was considered their ship. For the less privileged, however, it was much more difficult to get on board, for the Party bureaucracy maintained control and turned away those who were not considered suitable. Even Commander Hugo Heydel, a senior officer with the 9th Escort Division with responsibility for protecting the convoys, was unable to get places for his family on the liner.

To the submariners, their families and friends, and to the women auxiliaries and wounded soldiers, the *Gustloff* seemed to offer a safe and comfortable passage west. To the pressing thousands of refugees from the East who had suffered grotesque hardships to get to Gdynia at all she represented the final hope. Held back from the gangways by armed sentries, men and women who had already lost everything but their lives pleaded to get the specially printed passes. Those with money were prepared to pay anything; and those without were ready to fight to get on to the ship.

"There must have been 60,000 people on the docks and as soon as we let down the gangways people raced forward and pushed their way in," said Walter Knust. "In the confusion a lot of children got separated from their parents. Either the kids got on board leaving their parents on the harbour or the children were left behind as their parents got pushed forward by the throng."

The precious pieces of paper, printed in Gothic type on the ship's own press which in peacetime had provided its special newspaper and menus, were headed: "Identity Pass for MS *Wilhelm Gustloff*". They carried the stamp of the headquarters of the U-boat Training Division along with the owner's name and reason for being on board. U-boat personnel claimed them as of right for their families; refugees with local and Nazi Party influence schemed for them; and those with money tried to buy them. In the early stages those who had managed to acquire passes went aboard in orderly fashion, while the refugees packed on the quay looked at them with bitter envy. But as thousands more refugees poured into the dock area the tension mounted, and the *Wilhelm Gustloff* was tugged a few metres away from the quay to prevent the refugees rushing the gangways or sneaking aboard during the night. Those with passes boarded a ferry at the other side of the harbour and climbed a guarded gangway on the starboard, seaward side.

Fritz Brustat-Naval, a distinguished writer on naval subjects and a wartime Commander in the navy, was present and he vividly described the scene to the authors. "You really had to fight a way through to the ships. I remember forcing a way through with a squad of wounded soldiers who were being evacuated and when we got there the ship was still very bureaucratic and passes had to be shown.

"The whole area was full of refugees and cluttered with horse-drawn covered wagons which had brought them thousands of miles through the snow. What I remember best was all the horses and dogs which had come overland with the treks and had been abandoned by their owners because they had nothing to feed them on. They were all over the city centre and the dock area."

Baroness Ebbi von Maydell felt nothing but relief on getting aboard the liner. A Lithuanian by birth, she was the widow of a German aristocrat and since 1939 had lived in Gydnia where she ran a perfume boutique. She had the good fortune to be the friend of Professor Adolf Bock, an artist who specialised in marine drawings and paintings and had lived on board the *Wilhelm Gustloff* for several years as a kind of official war artist with a cabin of his own on the Command Deck.

He had used his influence to get passes for the Baroness and her two sons. But the elder boy, sixteen-year-old Bernard, refused to go. He argued that the sea was full of Russian submarines and far too dangerous. Instead, he decided to make the journey overland. The Baroness and her younger son, thirteen-year-old Gunther, remember going through two checkpoints where they had to show their passes on the gangway and then they were taken to a small cabin, No. 40 on the Upper Promenade Deck, which they shared with another woman and her daughter. They were delighted to be installed on the liner, and most grateful to Professor Bock.

The Baroness had felt a sense of impending doom ever since Christmas, which they had celebrated in austere but traditional fashion in their comfortable family home. Then they had all sat together for the last time, dining by candlelight in a room hung with the portraits of ancestors and with old blue English plates. The city was full of talk of the advancing Russians. There were daily air raids and water and electricity supplies had broken down. And yet it did not seem possible that Germany could lose Prussia. Surely the Teutonic Knights would rise and slaughter the barbarians as they had done so long ago? Surely the spirit of old Field Marshal von Hindenburg, who crushed the invading Russians at Tannenberg in 1914, and was buried with his wife on the battlefield, would come to their aid? It was not to be. Hindenburg's body was carried away from Königsberg at the last moment by the cruiser *Emden*. And Königsberg itself, symbol of eighteenth-century Prussian enlightenment, was to be destroyed by the Russians and turned into a fishing village.

So the von Maydells, like so many thousands of others, left their home and trudged through the snow to the docks. At least they had a cabin and were thankful for this privilege, for they were aware of the discomfort of thousands of others who poured into the ship. Already, only a day after they had gone aboard, the liner seemed to be overflowing with humanity. They found themselves impatiently asking when the ship would sail.

That night, January 27th, they were woken by an air-raid warning. Everybody was told to go ashore. "We barely managed to find protection in one of the three overcrowded shelters in the port," Gunther recalled. "Later we heard there had been a big raid on Danzig and that many refugees had been killed."

Gunther, who now lives in Hamburg, was excited to be on board ship. He enjoyed reading boys' adventure stories and now here he was, part of an adventure himself. He had dragged the family's few precious possessions and three suit-cases on a sledge through the snow, and once on board he began exploring. Prudently, he took a look at the lifeboats. There should have been twenty-two hung from the davits, eleven on either side of the Sun Deck. But a number of the davits were empty and nobody seemed to be doing anything to the boats that remained. They were full of snow and their launch-ing ropes looked frozen to their pulleys. It was a detail which few of the other refugees, delighted with the warmth and security of the ship, bothered to notice.

A sixteen-year-old girl named Eva Luck recorded in her diary how she went on board:

Early this morning we left our apartment in Gdynia. As we went out the sky seemed very high because when I looked up I could see millions of transparent white snowflakes. We all walked to the harbour, my mother and father and my little six-year-old sister, Dorrit. A terrible long way.

An icy wind tore at our coats and brought tears to our eyes. Dorrit cried because she was so cold and my father scolded her, but it was only because he was so worried. They would not let him come with us and he had to leave us at the place where we got on to a little boat taking us to the ship. Only the day before he had got passes for us. I was frightened I would get seasick on the little boat. Mummy was in despair.

They had to show their papers and boarding passes to get into the harbour. All the cabins were full already, and the family were told they would have to stay in the music room on the liner during the short voyage.

"A nice sailor gave me a little dark blue lifejacket which matched my wool dress," wrote Eva.

There was a lot of noise and soon they called us to lunch. We got a nice stew, but we had to hurry because there was another group queuing for their turn.

Then with some schoolfriends I set out to explore the ship. We looked into the big rooms and ran through long corridors until we got lost. Then an officer showed us the way back. It was a pity Daddy could not come with us, saying goodbye made him so sad. Otherwise I should have enjoyed it. I had never been on a big ship before.

Frau Paula Maria Knust, then aged twenty-three, was an early arrival on board. She had no difficulty in getting one of the coveted passes, for her then husband Walter, the second engineer, had spent two years aboard the liner. He considered himself lucky to get the posting. As a Merchant Navy officer he had been incorporated in the naval service when war broke out, and had been posted as engineer officer to the liner *Pretoria*. This ship was sent to Antwerp. The rumour aboard was that they were going to put her on the long and dangerous run made by some German ships to Japan. As Walter was the last surviving male member of his family, he benefited from a German wartime law which said that men in this position might be excused war service. His mother had written to the authorities and he was promptly transferred, first to Hamburg and then to the *Gustloff* lying in Gdynia. He was already there when Captain Petersen arrived to take command at the end of 1943.

Walter and Paula had an apartment in Gdynia, but as things ashore got worse she took to spending more and more time aboard ship.

She had been sent to Gdynia from her home in Mannheim

to work in a munitions factory but had then joined the Women's Naval Auxiliaries in which she became a group leader in charge of 100 girls serving in offices and on gunsites in order to release men for the front line. She was responsible for discipline and teaching the girls how to use pistols. But then she met Walter Knust and left the service when she married in 1944. Her life began to centre round the *Gustloff* and she became part of the permanent community on board the liner. However, she maintained her contacts with the Auxiliaries and saw her friends coming aboard in the later stages of the embarkation.

Some of them had to fight their way through the throng of refugees, and she was pleased to learn that they had been settled comfortably below decks in the drained swimming pool, each provided with a comfortable mattress. "By the time they came on board it was all panic," she said. She was delighted to see Professor Bock, a familiar face, among the crowd of new-comers and stopped to chat with him. Frau Knust shared her husband's cabin on B Deck where he had easy access to the engine room. She therefore saw more of the crew than she did of the refugees and remembers that, after taking on thousands of passengers and the stores to look after them, they were be-coming impatient for orders to sail.

Captains Weller and Kohler were getting anxious. They wanted to get this voyage over and done with because the atmosphere between the Merchant Navy officers and the sub-mariners was becoming increasingly sour and they did not like the way matters were going. The Merchant Navy officers tended to keep to themselves. They lunched in their own cabins, while the submarine officers ate together in the ward-room. Tentatively, the two captains joined the naval officers for lunch on their first day aboard and found their welcome formal rather than friendly.

It was, moreover, far from clear even at this late stage how the responsibilities and the command were to be divided, although Weller and Kohler had been instructed before leaving Hamburg that the duty officer of the watch would be responsible for all executive sailing orders. As Captain Petersen was considered ill qualified to handle the liner at sea, they would be responsible for sailing the ship, though without full powers of command.

One of the problems which worried them was that there were still very few seamen on board. In particular, there was a serious shortage of petty officers and senior ratings, the men who make a ship work. Only two elderly bosuns could be found. Weller and Kohler felt relieved therefore when three young officers, borrowed from other ships in the harbour, arrived to help the scratch team which was going to take the 25,000-ton liner with thousands of people on board through the dangerous waters of the Baltic.

Zahn took it upon himself to lecture the ship's officers on the naval situation. He expressed his confidence that they would not need to worry about enemy warships and submarines. He was, however, apprehensive about having to sail through newly sown minefields and the possibility of attacks from the air.

He became furious when he discovered that anti-aircraft guns had not yet been mounted because there were no dockhands to man the cranes, and Polish workers were refusing to help. He spotted a floating crane being towed by tugs and shouted through a loud-hailer to the Poles on board: "I have ten bottles of schnapps for you if you help swing these guns on board." It was an offer the Poles couldn't refuse, and shortly the guns were being hoisted into position.

Grey naval trucks were kept busy bringing provisions for the ship which was already feeding 4,000 people on board. Every passenger was to get one hot meal a day. Though not much, this was a luxury for many, who had enjoyed no such plenty for weeks. Thirty carcasses of pork were taken on board along with tons of flour to keep the ship's bakers busy at the bread ovens.

With two days to go before she sailed, the *Wilhelm Gustloff* still had only twelve lifeboats. The others had been requisitioned by the Harbourmaster for special duties in the port during the long period when the ship had been immobile. When the air raids had started earlier in the war the port defence officer began laying smoke screens in the harbour to make things more difficult for attacking aircraft. He had used lifeboats from the *Gustloff* and other liners to chug around the port making smoke. So ten of the big lifeboats, which Walter Knust told us had diesel engines and were capable of taking up to 120 passengers, were missing at this crucial moment.

However, by raiding stores and other ships, the authorities managed to gather together eighteen small boats, most of them cutters; heavy-oared craft normally used for giving elementary sea training to U-boat cadets. These boats were lifted on to the Sun Deck and lashed down ready to be quickly released in an emergency.

A number of naval rafts were also stacked on the upper decks. Painted red, white and grey, they were made of sheet steel over buoyancy tanks and were stacked in piles at convenient points. Orders had also gone out for every passenger to be issued with a lifejacket. Lorries brought these to the dockside together with piles of mattresses for the refugees to sleep on.

And so the work of preparing the *Wilhelm Gustloff* for her first cruise in nearly five years went on – in hurried but, considering the difficulties, well-organised fashion.

In the early hours of January 29th yet another ambulance train arrived in Gdynia. The wounded it carried were to be embarked during the day and the ship's doctor, Dr. Richter, worked through the morning preparing a sick bay in the Arbour, the glass-fronted observation lounge at the front of the Sun Deck, and making the new arrivals as comfortable as possible. Many of them had dreadful wounds and it seemed unlikely that they would live through the voyage.

Similar preparations were taking place a few hundred metres away on another liner, the *Hansa*. She was taking on board officers of the U-boat Divisions, wounded soldiers and refugees, and the two ships were to sail as part of the same convoy. It was now obvious that the order to sail must be imminent. Every day, every hour, brought news of fresh disasters at the front.

Those already in the *Gustloff* were constantly lectured over the public address system on what to do in an emergency. There were the customary instructions on how to put on life-jackets, and a number of drills were carried out. At eleven a.m. on January 29th the bridge practised the emergency drills for closing the water-tight bulkheads. "Attention, attention!" said the officer of the watch. "This is an exercise. We are closing all water-tight doors. Attention, please! When you hear the alarm bell sound three times at short intervals the drill will begin."

It was at this moment that a messenger arrived with a signal for Zahn from Captain Schütze, the officer commanding U-boats. The *Gustloff* was to be ready to sail the following day. The message, passed on to Captain Petersen by Commander Zahn, brought relief on the bridge, for the officers were keenly aware of the frustration of their crew, the growing tension of the passengers packed below decks, and the resentment of all those refugees on the quay who had not managed to acquire an "Identity Pass for MS *Wilhelm Gustloff*".

But at the headquarters of the 9th Escort Division, which would be responsible for convoying the big ships to safety, the sailing orders caused a great deal of anxiety.

IO

THE MAN WITH overall responsibility for what the German naval historian, Professor Jürgen Rohwer described as "the greatest evacuation operation in history" was Admiral Kummetz, German Naval High Commander, East. In January 1945 he was faced with the task of organising the sea rescue of millions of refugees, the transfer of the U-boat Training Divisions, and the movement of soldiers and wounded from the Eastern Front. He was handicapped by the limited naval forces at his disposal, by shortage of fuel, and by complete lack of air cover. In addition, he had to go on supplying the German Army still holding on to outlying positions.

In the winter of early 1945 the German Navy had two convoy protection units in being in the area. In the East was the 9th Escort Division commanded by Commander Adalbert von Blanc, later promoted to Rear Admiral, whose area stretched from the Gulf of Danzig to Courland. The area from Rixhöft on the coast west of Danzig as far west as the Danish islands was the domain of the 10th Escort Division, commanded from February onwards by Commander Hugo Heydel, who until then had been based in Gdynia.

The 9th Escort Division was composed largely of three flotillas of minesweepers, each with half a dozen operational ships, two flotillas of motor minesweepers and an assortment of converted trawlers and small fishery vessels. Its neighbouring division, the 10th, with whom liaison was especially close because Heydel and von Blanc were old friends, had a similar force at its disposal.

More powerful warships, such as destroyers and torpedo boats which were attached to the two task forces of capital ships formed by Admiral Doenitz to harass the advancing Red Army from the sea, operated separately. From time to time escort destroyers and torpedo boats were used for other purposes, including the evacuation of troops and refugees. At this stage the most formidable obstacle to the evacuation was not the Red Banner Fleet but the Royal Air Force. In January the RAF dropped 668 mines which sank eighteen ships and the following month laid 1,345 mines. They concentrated on the area round Swinemunde, headquarters of the 10th Escort Division, but they also operated as far east as the coast of Pomerania, causing long delays to the convoys while the mines were swept.

The Soviet submarine offensive concentrated at first on the route to Courland which was the scene of intensive German naval and supply ship activity in support of the pockets of Germans still fighting on, although the Red Army had reached many miles beyond them. However, a number of large Soviet submarines also operated individually in the area between Rixhöft and Bornholm. Fortunately for the Germans the Soviet Air Force was still heavily involved in land operations when the evacuation started, and therefore had little potential for operations against the ships.

The escort division officers in Gdynia and Danzig were all aware of the danger the *Gustloff* and the other ocean liners would run as they made their way along the Pomeranian coast. The risk of mines limited their choice of course. Defences against submarine attack were inadequate because the escorts had no effective anti-submarine vessels with modern equipment until the second half of February, when two submarine-chaser flotillas were moved into the area.

It was in such conditions that the naval officers in their sandbagged headquarters on the threatened coast around Danzig had to plan the movement westwards of a whole fleet of liners. "This last task came upon us suddenly and it grew much faster than we thought possible," said Commander Hugo Heydel who, from his headquarters in Swinemunde, became responsible for the protection of convoys in the sector most vulnerable to submarine attack and to the RAF's mine-laying operations. He and his fellow commanders performed a brilliant feat of improvisation in desperate circumstances. Their difficulties were manifold. The navy was operating far from its main base in Kiel. Because of the shortage of war-ships, it was necessary to use almost everything that would float. Fuel was rapidly running out. And the Russians were overrunning their bases – Admiral von Blanc was forced to move his 9th Division Headquarters from Libau back to Pillau.

That was the gloomy state of affairs when Rear Admiral Engelhardt, Wehrmacht Naval Transport Commander, placed at the disposal of the great evacuation fourteen liners, varying in size between the 9,554-ton *Ubena* and the *Cap Arkona*, 27,564 tons. In addition, the evacuation commanders had available twenty-three freighters of more than 5,000 tons and many other smaller ships.

Had it not been for the perspicacity of Admiral Engelhardt the evacuation plan could never have succeeded, for he had anticipated the need to pull out troops and refugees by sea and had begun earmarking ships in the autumn of 1944. Doenitz, whose attitude at that stage was ambiguous, never-theless gave him a free hand; and Engelhardt used the Gross Admiral's authority to override the objections of Nazi officials who dreaded that they would be accused of defeatism if they became involved in evacuation projects. He also coped with shipowners who did not want their ships to be used in such dangerous operations until it had been arranged who would pay for damage caused by carrying soldiers and refugees.

But while preparations were being made at high level, with orders going out to dockyards to concentrate on the repair and maintenance of evacuation ships, there was much inter-ference at lower levels. Gauleiter Koch, for example, regularly made his men comb the shipyards for able-bodied workers to serve in his private army and many who would have been more usefully employed at their normal jobs were taken away under threat of death.

In any case it was rather late to reorganise shipbuilding programmes. It was one of the ironies of war that for years the resources of Hitler's Reich had been monopolised for the construction of submarines rather than for merchant vessels.

In this situation, much depended on the quality of the naval officers whose task it was to control loading and movements.

Great credit for the overall success of the operation must be given to Commander Heinrich Bartels, the fifty-five-year-old naval officer whose unenviable task it was to organise merchant ships and crews to carry the refugees to safety. He was expected not only to summon up ships but also to supervise the embarkation of the groups huddling, frozen and half-starved, on every quayside between Gdynia and Pillau. He had his headquarters in the old-fashioned Strand Hotel, now showing the neglect of war, and his official position was that of operations officer to Admiral Theodor Burchardi, Senior Naval Officer, Eastern Baltic.

Bartels was a sailor with a long experience of the sea and of warfare. He had started his professional life in the Merchant Navy and then, as a very young man, was called up in the First World War. After the war he served as a civilian in the naval supply service before becoming a regular naval officer in the mid-1930s. In the Second World War he had seen action in the Gulf of Finland. He had witnessed the German disasters at Leningrad and the abandonment of the Finnish bases. He had been responsible for evacuating soldiers and stores as the army retreated ever westwards and now, a veteran of the retreat from Latvia and Estonia and the evacuation by sea of Riga and Reval, he probably knew more about the embarkation and supply of large bodies of men than any other officer in the German Navy. At one stage he had been responsible for the whole supply line of the army in

Courland. He was a hustler, and yet was popular with both sailors and senior officers. He was described by an old friend as "a good guy, a man who did not spit into the beer".

When he first arrived in Danzig on a mission from Admiral Burchardi, he found the port commander overwhelmed by the size of the refugee problem and his office the scene of hysterical and useless conferences. Confident that he could order affairs in a more businesslike fashion, Bartels decided to set up shop in Gdynia, a move authorised by his Admiral and then confirmed by Admiral Doenitz, who ordered him to stay in the Bay of Danzig area and to organise the evacuation of East and West Prussia "should that become necessary". When Doenitz ordered the submariners to flee, that moment had obviously arrived.

It took a man of great force and determination to organise the evacuation. Bartels was precisely the man for the job. He set to work to weed out the incompetent officers and those who had cracked under the strain. He seemed to revel in a fight, taking on the Nazi Party, the shipowners, the army, anyone who stood in his path. On one occasion, as people were being marshalled for embarkation, he strode through the crowd to sort things out. A column of troops had just drawn up at the quayside. He went up to their officers and declared: "You are not to come aboard. This ship is for the wounded and for refugees. Your orders are to stay here and fight."

His task became so difficult that Admiral Burchardi moved to Gdynia in order to add his authority to that of his subordinate.

But neither Burchardi nor Bartels, nor any of the other officers engaged in convoy or evacuation work, had any control over the submarine service. They were a law unto themselves. Hugo Heydel told the authors that at that time the submarine service was often called the "5th Wehrmachtsteil" (Fifth Arm of the Forces). They regarded themselves as an élite, waiting only for the arrival of their new submarines, the wonder weapons, with which they would strike stunning blows at the enemy. They enjoyed high prestige in Hitler's eyes and were protected by the patronage of Doenitz.

It may be that they were whistling in the dark. They had taken a terrible beating in the Atlantic and when they went on patrol after 1943 the odds were against their coming home. J. P. Mallman Showell, whose father died in U 377, reports in his book *U-Boats under the Swastika* that he "never heard of an ex-U-boat man who actually enjoyed going to sea after 1940. Had the men been given the choice to go home or to stay with the U-boats then Hitler would have been left with just a handful of fanatics. The new recruits joining the U-Boat Arm were keen to fight, but this was due to the propaganda with which they had been indoctrinated, and not to hearing depth charges explode."

Mr. Mallmann Showell goes on to report that

there was a noticeable change in the U-Boat men's attitude from 1944 onwards. On arrival at the office the shore-based staff started to say "Good Morning" instead of the obligatory "Heil Hitler". Songs such as *"Denn wir fahren gegen Engeland"* (We are sailing against England) or U 47's hymn *"So klein ist das Boot und so gross ist das Meer"* (So small is the boat and so large is the sea) were being replaced by far more cynical songs that lamented the poor weapons of the U-Boats and the radar that was being used to hunt them. The men knew they were beaten and that their end was inevitable – but no one knew how long Germany would last and there was always a faint glimmer of hope in Hitler's promises of new weapons.

When Petty Officer Hans Schottes arrived to take a submarine training course with the 2nd U-Boat Training Division, he reported aboard the *Gustloff* to Lieutenant Dankel whom he had known as a short course university student in Berlin. Dankel, unfit for sea duty because an injury compelled him to wear a glass eye, was incredulous at the news that Schottes had actually volunteered for submarine duties. "You must be mad to go into those 'coffins'," he said; and assumed that Schottes must have got some girl into trouble.

But it must be remembered that the training divisions were strictly disciplined and existed to instil esprit de corps into the recruits. Instructors worked hard on the *Gustloff* to convince the U-boat cadets that they were better than anybody else in the navy. It was this certainty of superiority which conditioned the submariners' attitude to all things and now they were under orders to withdraw from the Gulf of Danzig, they were going to leave in their own ships and do things their own way.

Therefore, inevitably, there was no liaison between those in charge of the submariners' ship *Wilhelm Gustloff* and the officer in charge of organising the convoys of big ships now preparing to sail across the Baltic. This was Commander Wolfgang Leonhardt, a much decorated officer with long experience of action against the Russians in the Eastern Baltic. He was head of the 9th Escort Division in Gdynia. He had a small office on the wide quay between Bay One and Bay Two on the harbour. To help him in the map and radio room he had five officers and a handful of ratings, yet with these modest resources he had responsibility for a naval parish stretching 700 nautical miles, and responsibility for the fate of thousands of people and dozens of ships. As the convoys and the groups of minesweepers moved, Leonhardt plotted their positions and stuck small flags along the "safe paths" organised for them.

While the *Wilhelm Gustloff* was preparing for sea he had already despatched the first big liner convoy to the West. The *Robert Ley*, 27,288 tons, the *Pretoria*, 16,662 tons – which had not, after all, made the run to Japan – and the *Ubena*, with a total of 7,000 refugees on board left Pillau, and under the management of the Escort Division made the voyage safely to West German ports. Commander Leonhardt had also

73

arranged a fast convoy of two modern freighters, the *Minden* and the *Cometa*, carrying 2,500 troops with an escort of one torpedo boat and two minesweepers. But the queen of the fleet of evacuation liners gathered to carry out the big operation was the *Wilhelm Gustloff*; and she belonged to the submariners.

Because of the intense activity now afoot, Commander Leonhardt in his comfortless office on the dockside found that on the morning of January 30th, 1945 all his ships were at sea. He had not one single escort vessel at his disposal in Gdynia. Yet Leonhardt was responsible for coordinating the movement of convoys and passing them on to Commander Heydel, who controlled the area west of the Gulf of Danzig. Heydel, too, was experiencing exactly the same difficulties. "By that time the situation had become one of total panic as the refugees kept pouring in and swamping the organisation," he told us.

Within sight of Leonhardt's headquarters lay the *Cap Arkona*, the once-proud flagship of the Hamburg-Süd line which had plied between Hamburg and South America. She was besieged by refugees and eventually took on board the staggering total of 14,000. The Commander estimated that he would not feel happy sending her to sea with less than half a dozen minesweepers as escort. At Danzig was the *Deutschland* with 12,000 people. The two ships together had taken on the equivalent of the population of a small town. In addition to that there were the *Deutschland*'s big sister ships, the *Hansa* and the *Hamburg*. Yet there were no warships to escort them.

Commander Leonhardt decided that it would be totally irresponsible to send these ships to sea unescorted. He knew that Soviet submarines were going on the offensive, for they had already sunk two coasters off Memel, and it was to be expected that before long they would penetrate the Gulf of Danzig.

The *Cap Arkona*, and indeed all the other liners, had reported their readiness to leave to Commander Leonhardt in correct naval fashion. He acknowledged their signals, and instructed them to stand by until escorts could be arranged for a proper convoy. Things were very different with regard to the *Gustloff* and the *Hansa*, both under the control of the 2nd U-Boat Training Division with its shore headquarters in Bay Nine on the Oxhöft side of the port.

Leonhardt only heard by chance that the *Gustloff* was nearly ready for sea. One of his subordinates had happened to pass the ship, and had noticed the activity on board.

Commander Leonhardt rang Training Division Headquarters and asked about their plans. He was told that the *Gustloff* would sail within twenty-four hours. He then asked what escort arrangements had been made, and the officer taking the call said that he did not know anything about that. As a result of this telephone call Captain Schütze, commander of the submarine division, invited Commander Leonhardt to a conference at his headquarters.

In his excellent book on the evacuation from the Baltic, *Flucht übers Meer,* Cajus Bekker, the well-known German author, recounted in these words what happened as a U-boat officer began the proceedings with a briefing. "We have orders to move our accommodation ships, *Wilhelm Gustloff* and *Hansa,* to the West. Embarkation is almost completed and they are now ready to sail." The Captain then asked the Escort Division for information about routes and hostile forces.

Leonhardt was amazed, for nothing seemed to have been planned in advance. And it suddenly dawned on him that his U-boat colleagues were seriously thinking of sending out these two big liners without protection. He began his customary briefing on the latest mine situation, then stopped in mid-sentence.

"At this moment I am not in a position to provide your ships with adequate protection," he warned. "In a few days that situation will change and then the Convoy Commander will have full and up-to-date reports about enemy movements and routes to be taken."

Captain Schütze replied: "I am afraid we cannot wait until

you arrange a convoy. The sooner we leave the better." For a moment the two officers, both with excellent war records in their particular branch of the naval service, confronted each other. Commander Leonhardt was forced to yield despite his conviction that the submariners were being irresponsible. He was outranked by Captain Schütze.

The psychology of the submarine service played an important part in this conflict of opinion. Bekker notes that for the U-boat officers, the Atlantic, not the Baltic, was the place for serious warfare. For nearly five years they had been involved in fierce battles attacking British convoys in face of the best convoy defence system ever organised. In their view the Baltic was an adventure playground by comparison, a sea area where new crews and captains learned the elementary tricks of their trade. It was not a place for fight-to-the-death engagements, for the Russian fleet had made little impact on the German Navy and supply convoys had been running in and out without interference from the Soviet Navy.

Commander Leonhardt had a completely different perspective. As commander of the 25th Minesearching Flotilla he had been at the sharp end of German naval operations on the East Sea Front, patrolling the mine barriers in Narwa Bay. He knew how tenaciously the Russians could fight at sea.

He was seriously worried, therefore, by the decision of the Submarine Training Division to go it alone. As soon as he returned to his office after the meeting at submarine headquarters, he called von Blanc, the senior Escort Division officer, and reported what was happening. His commander agreed with him that liners with so many people on board should not be allowed to leave without a proper escort, and that their sailing should be controlled by the Escort Division.

Cajus Bekker in his account of the dispute reported Commander Leonhardt making this point: "But they will sail, Sir. How am I to stop them? All they have is a symbolic escort of a few of their own ships."

Von Blanc promised that he would do all he could to prevent the departure of unescorted ships. He said that he would report on the situation at once to the Naval Command for the Eastern Baltic. He even took the matter up with Naval Headquarters in Berlin, asking for their authorisation to stop the *Gustloff*.

Meanwhile the submariners remained adamant; they had their orders to sail, and they intended to carry them out no matter what the Escort Division officers recommended. Moreover, they argued, they were able to provide their own escort, for attached to them were several torpedo boats as well as an array of small warships, normally used for towing targets, mine hunters and torpedo recovery vessels. While von Blanc waited for replies to his signals to Kiel and Berlin, Captain Schütze went ahead with his plans, ignoring the arguments of the convoy officers that once the liners weighed anchor to set sail for the West they should come under the jurisdiction of the Escort Divisions.

Cajus Bekker poses the question, who was right in this argument? He then quotes Admiral Doenitz saying after the war: "During their exercises the submarine training divisions operated independently of the control of escort forces. But at the moment when they were ordered to move West their transport was like any other, and was clearly the responsibility of Admiral Burchardi. Under these circumstances the 9th Escort Division was responsible for their movement."

But this cool, considered judgment did not prevail in the over-heated atmosphere of Gdynia. The submariners went their own way and their actions filled Commander Leonhardt with foreboding. Nor did this dispute between naval officers do anything to improve relations between the naval and Merchant Navy officers aboard the *Wilhelm Gustloff*.

On the Boat Deck of the liner more personal anxieties prevailed. Louis Reese was busy with a party of deckhands struggling to clear the thick layer of ice and snow which young Gunther von Maydell had noticed in the lifeboats during his reconnaissance when he first went on board. Reese was approached by a member of the ship's company, Eugen Jeissle, the head printer. Jeissle wanted permission for his wife and new-born baby to come on board. Reese told him that any member of the crew could bring his family on board, but added that he did not advise it. If it was his own wife, he said, he would find another way of getting her to safety. "I don't like it," he added.

The printer ignored the advice. He had printed the passes admitting others and felt perhaps that it was only proper to use some to admit his own family.

Down in his *salon de coiffure*, the ship's barber, happy to be leaving Gdynia, was doing a roaring trade as the refugees tried to improve their appearance. Even at a time of disaster, people still need their hair cut. His worry was that he had heard ashore that there was a plan to devalue the currency and he might lose money on his tips. For this reason he had prudently stored five-Deutschmark pieces which he had heard were bound to keep their value, because they were silver. He prepared for an emergency by acquiring a rucksack into which they could be stowed if he had to move in a hurry.

I I

FEW OF THE passengers knew that the ship would sail the following day. Some had already been on board for three or four days, and were impatient to leave as the ominous rumbling of the Russian artillery and the frightening wail of the rockets from the Stalin Organs grew closer. The ship was already full and by evening there was a feeling of growing anxiety. Why were they still waiting? Then a rumour spread, that it was too late to sail and the Russians were expected at any minute. Frightened men and women whispered that they would all be put ashore that night and formed in to suicide squads to defend Gdynia to the end against the invaders. The Purser's office was besieged by passengers trying to find out what was happening. Eventually, reassurance came in an announcement read over the public address system: "The *Wilhelm Gustloff* is ready for sea. We shall be leaving to-morrow."

The loading of equipment continued throughout the night, while a fresh stream of refugees arrived on the docks as word of the impending departures spread through the town. Efforts to get on board became more frantic. Women tried to smuggle their husbands and sons on to the ships, disguising them as women or hiding them in trunks while SS squads patrolled among the crowds in search of men suitable for pressing into war service.

This was a time of anguished decision for Nazi Party officials in the region. Here was the *Wilhelm Gustloff*, a party ship with the Swastika-shaped insignia of the Strength Through Joy movement still faintly showing on her funnel, ready to sail to safety. Party influence could get them places on board, but if their decision was noticed by Gauleiter Koch, and brought to the attention of Himmler or Hitler, they would be branded as cowards and defeatists who could expect no mercy. But against that, what mercy could they expect from the Red Army? The Germans had slaughtered every Communist Party official they captured. The men of the Nazi Party could expect no kinder fate.

On the liner, the Führer suite on B Deck had been kept empty until the 29th – "Reserved for VIPs". Then the Burgomeister of Gdynia brought his family on board to occupy it, thirteen people in all. The unfortunate functionary did not dare to remain with them and made his way ashore next day. He died fighting in defence of his city. Other distinguished last-minute passengers arrived the same night to cram themselves into an officer's cabin on the top deck: the Kreisleiter of Gdynia, his wife and five children, a maid and a parlour maid.

The last cabin to be filled was the office of Herr Kaufhold, the pre-war Nazi Party group leader of the ship. In this emergency even that holy of holies had to be sacrificed. Yet still at this juncture some Party members and especially their wives had the face to complain about their crowded quarters.

And in truth, though there was some over-crowding in the cabins, the ship had space for more people. The other liners belonging to the submariners, the *Hansa*, the *Hamburg*, and the *Deutschland*, all smaller than the *Gustloff*, had each managed to take on board 7,000 passengers. Because the *Gustloff* was a special ship, a Party ship, she had taken fewer than the others.

In usefulness rather than in rank or party standing the most important of the late arrivals was a twenty-one-year-old leading telegraphist of the naval signal branch. He was Rudi Lange who had been sent to take over the radio room of the liner. The fact that he was needed at all showed how short of trained crew the liner was.

And so the hours ticked away while last-minute preparations were made. In an effort to cheer up the 162 wounded soldiers in their emergency hospital in the Arbour, Dr. Richter got together a small orchestra to play to them. If the music failed to do much for morale, at least it drowned the moans of the wounded. Not far away, on the Sun Deck, the sailors had set up a special maternity ward, for a number of the women refugees were heavily pregnant.

While all this was going on the fanatical Gauleiter Koch – who, as we have revealed earlier, had made his own escape plans – was still delivering his hard-line speeches urging people to fight on until Hitler chose to use his secret weapons and throw the Russians back. There were still a few who believed him.

Ashore, Hans Joachim Paris, a German war correspondent broadcasting from Königsberg, said the city "has become part of the front-line area. Thousands listen in the night to hear if the thunder of the battle is approaching the town. We have all got used to the sight of the automatic pistols and close-range anti-tank weapons on our tables and writing desks, ready to be taken up at a moment's notice. Volkssturm units drafted from offices and homesteads are being equipped with weapons to fight the tanks in the streets. To provide passage for reinforcements the streets have been cleared of the long treks of fugitives".

12

ON THE MORNING of Tuesday, January 30th, Commander Zahn rose early and not long after the new dawn took Hassan for a brisk walk along the quay. The dog was devoted to him and even on such a dramatic day Zahn felt that he should be given his normal exercise. Few people on the *Wilhelm Gustloff* had slept that night, the atmosphere was too strained and the rumours too worrying. The quay along which the U-boat officer strode in his long leather coat was crowded with tired, half-frozen refugees who looked enviously at early-rising passengers on the ship's decks, wishing that they too were on board, with safety from the Russians virtually guaranteed.

Zahn was conscious of the rising tension and at about nine o'clock he telephoned U-boat headquarters to find out when the ship would sail – for the sailing time was U-boat business and nothing to do with Escort Division. Captain Schütze replied that it would probably be midday, although no definite time had yet been arranged. At a neighbouring berth the *Hansa* which was to sail with the *Gustloff*, was still taking on refugees at the insistence of Commander Bartels. In the course of the conversation Zahn said that he had about 4,500 refugees already on board and could take no more. In reply to another question about hostile naval movements, headquarters again told him that they had no reports of Soviet submarines.

As the morning wore on there were signs that the liner would indeed sail soon. At ten a.m. military police boarded the ship to search for deserters, but they went away empty-handed. A little later the pilot who was to take the ship out of the harbour went up on to the bridge. U-boat headquarters had insisted that the pilot be German, for Poles could not be relied upon and might inform the Russians about the movements of the ships. Four tugs came alongside and Zahn made his final call to U-boat headquarters just before the telephone landline was hauled ashore.

"The *Gustloff* is to sail at twelve-thirty," they told him, "and she will probably have to make for Stettin."

In a macabre parody of their peacetime function, the ship's loudspeakers constantly relayed information and instructions to the passengers, calling them to meals one deck at a time, making lost children appeals and reiterating the order that all passengers must wear lifejackets at all times. "No smoking below decks," ordered the bridge. "Attention, attention, no light must be shown after an air-raid alert has been signalled."

At about 1200 hours the sea dutymen closed up, hatches were secured and deckhands stood by the moorings fore and aft. Finally just before the gangways were hauled inboard, the ship's manifest in quintriplicate was handed down to the Harbour Master's launch alongside. Despite the emergency, despite the drama of the situation, everything was being done by the book as the *Wilhelm Gustloff* prepared to make her first trip to sea for nearly five years. The aged Captain Petersen was a stickler for correct dress and behaviour. New members of the crew were warned to wear their caps because "the Old Man doesn't like people going about naked on the *Gustloff*".

Similar departure routines were taking place aboard the *Hansa*, and the other liners, the *Hamburg* and the *Deutschland*. But nowhere were they carried out with more punctilio than on the bridge of the *Gustloff*. The final act on the bridge was for Purser Luth officially to hand over to First Officer Reese the complete passenger list. He glanced at it just to check the figures. They were:

> 918 Naval officers and men
> 173 Crew
> 373 Women's Naval Auxiliaries
> 162 Wounded
> 4,424 Refugees

Thus, at that time, there were 6,050 people recorded as being aboard the *Gustloff*.

Last-minute efforts had provided the ship with enough life-jackets for everyone but there were still not enough lifeboats. Ten of the davits remained empty. A bosun named Gorch had taken a final look over the boats and reported there were still only twelve instead of the peacetime complement of twenty-two. He calculated that each of them had room for up to sixty people. Then there were the eighteen cutters which the navy had provided. These had room for thirty people each, and in addition there were 380 rafts for ten passengers each. According to these calculations this meant there was room in boats and rafts for 5,060 people.

It was nearly 1300 hours before the deckhands cast off and the four tugs began pulling the bows of the *Wilhelm Gustloff* away from the pier where she had lain for so long. She was forced to stop almost immediately, for a number of small boats drew alongside, each one filled with refugees, mostly women and children. They blocked the ship and from their crowded decks came pathetic shouts and appeals.

Women held up their children in their arms and implored: "Take us with you. Save the children!" Nobody could resist such cries. The liner drifted while the crew put out gangways and scrambling nets and the last-minute refugees, rewarded for their persistence, struggled on to the *Gustloff*. No one bothered to count them, for everyone was anxious to put to sea as soon as possible.

How many got aboard at this last moment is uncertain. Many years later, Rudi Lange told a reunion of survivors: "We put down nets and everybody on the small ships scrambled up as best they could. As we got under way I think I remember being told by one of the ship's officers to send a signal that another 2,000 people had come on board." If that was so, it meant that the *Gustloff* was carrying 8,000 people. But no one will ever know for certain.

Few of the passengers were hardy enough to stay on the

ship's rails as she eased away from the quay, for as the tugs pulled her stern out and her bows began swinging towards the harbour mouth a stiff north-west wind began bombarding her with hailstones. It was bitterly cold and there were gusts of snow unpleasant enough to prevent even Professor Bock, the naval artist, from observing the departure from on deck.

As the hail rattled against the glass panels of the bridge, Captain Petersen, who was still apprehensive about the danger of submarines, commented with relief on the bad weather which would help to hide the liner at sea.

"So far as I'm concerned," said Commander Zahn, "it would be even better if there was a pea soup fog." Now that the movement of the ship could be felt and the frustration of waiting anxiously for sailing orders was over, relations between the two officers on the bridge seemed to be improving. The mixed naval and merchant crew were starting to work together. There were naval ratings at the engine telegraphs and a naval quartermaster handled the wheel. They took their orders from the Merchant Navy Captain and officer of the watch.

As Captain Petersen watched through the snow-speckled window a naval minesweeper took up position ahead of the ship. The duty officer picked up the public address microphone and delivered a final message to the passengers below decks. "Attention, attention! All passengers must put on their lifejackets. From now on they must be worn at all times."

Because there were still so few lifeboats in the davits, the Captain had ordered the *Gustloff* to sail according to peace-time routine. That is to say, the boats were still inboard and not swung out on the davits. "It was a mistake," said Engineer Officer Knust later. "The boats should have been outboard because that was the wartime precaution for liners to be ready for emergencies."

The small naval craft patrolled ahead of the *Gustloff* on the look-out for mines just outside the great mole at the entrance to Gdynia harbour which the liner passed at 1300 hours. There was danger of mines dropped from marauding aircraft even as close to the great naval base as that.

The weather forecast was: West-North-West 6 to 7, turning West in the evening and dropping to 5. Swell 4, snow. Visibility 1–3 nautical miles, light to middling frost.

Gunther von Maydell had braved the hail to watch the ship's departure and he noticed with some surprise that there were lumps of ice floating on the sea.

Ashore at the headquarters of the 9th Escort Division, where the sailing of the *Gustloff* and the *Hansa* had caused so much anxiety, Commander Leonhardt was distracted from his worries about the convoy by other and more pressing tasks. At least it was a relief to be getting so many refugees away by sea. It would make more room on the docks and in the city for those still flocking in from more dangerous places like Königsberg.

13

EARLY IN THE afternoon a naval lieutenant rushed into Leonhardt's office waving a signal form. "*Gustloff* has dropped anchor. She waits for *Hansa*. *Hansa* has engine trouble."

It was a message which brought a degree of satisfaction to the convoy coordinator who was still convinced that U-boat headquarters had blundered in ordering the two big liners to sail without a properly organised screen of escorts. For despite the submariners confidence that they could provide their own escort, all that they had been able to scrape together were two small vessels, a torpedo boat and a torpedo recovery vessel. Leonhardt's reaction to the *Hansa*'s breakdown was that as the *Wilhelm Gustloff* would obviously not now sail alone, there would be more time to muster a stronger escort. But his satisfaction was short-lived, for within an hour another signal reported that the *Wilhelm Gustloff* had been ordered to leave the *Hansa* behind and sail on.

The original plan had been for the *Wilhelm Gustloff* and the *Hansa* to rendezvous off Hela where they would be picked up by the escort vessels provided by the submarine branch. But about an hour after sailing from Gdynia the look-outs on the *Gustloff* spotted the *Hansa* hove to not far from Hela. The *Gustloff* stopped too, and because the command had given strict orders for radio silence the bridge exchanged flag signals with the other liner, which reported she had engine trouble and relayed an order to the *Gustloff* – "You are to anchor here and stand by for further instructions".

Below decks the passengers, many of them seasick by this time, for the liner had begun to feel the full force of the wind and the sea, grew puzzled and then alarmed as the ship lost way. There was excited chatter about what this could mean. Frau Knust, the engineer's wife, remembers becoming anxious in her cabin and Baroness von Maydell, too, felt that something must have gone wrong. For the wounded in their glass-fronted hospital it felt like just one more trial they had to endure.

Captain Weller, who was on watch, tried to reassure the passengers over the loudhailer. "There is no cause for alarm. We shall be sailing again soon. Meanwhile make sure that your lifebelts are securely fastened."

There was no further explanation, and inevitably on such a crowded and anxious ship all manner of rumours quickly spread among the passengers. Tossed by the waves, the liner remained in this exposed position for about half an hour while the officers on the bridge waited to hear what had been decided for them by the Führer of Submarines.

There was little that Captain Schütze could do to help the *Hansa*. She would have to try to repair her own engines while tugs butted their way through the choppy sea to her assistance. But the naval command did not want to double the risk by keeping the *Gustloff* at anchor in daylight on this dangerous coast. Finally the decision was made and signalled to the *Hansa* who passed on the message by flag that she could not sail but that the *Gustloff* was to proceed alone. The master added a message of his own – "Bon voyage!"

Once again the *Gustloff* got under way. Commander Zahn was cursing up on the bridge for he did not like the way things were going, and neither he nor his Merchant Service colleagues were much reassured when they caught the first glimpse of their escort through the snow showers off Hela.

It consisted of an ancient torpedo boat called the *Löwe* (Lion), which had been captured by the Germans during the Norwegian Campaign in 1940, and a torpedo recovery vessel, the TF 19, whose only duty hitherto had been to hunt for practice torpedoes fired by the U-boat training crews.

Zahn had lamp signals made ordering these two sorry vessels to go ahead, one to port and one to starboard. "What an escort!" grumbled Captain Weller, who had taken over the watch. "We would have done better to wait for the *Hansa*."

Zahn replied that they had precise orders and must carry on.

By this time the *Gustloff* was beating into a short and rough sea which made life very difficult for the two small escort ships. The TF 19 was soon losing speed and before long the *Gustloff*'s yeoman of signals read off a lamp message from her: "Have crack along a welded seam and am making water. Must return to base."

There was nothing for it but to authorise her departure, one half of the escort of the flagship of the Strength Through Joy movement.

Only the *Löwe* was left, plunging and rolling ahead of the liner. This did nothing to help personal relations up on the bridge of the *Gustloff*. Commander Zahn, who felt the need for some initiative in these dire circumstances, entered into a tetchy argument with Captain Petersen over the correct course of action in the presence of the other officers, including the captains of the watch.

Zahn wanted to stick to the deep-water route westwards and as he saw it there were two possibilities. Either they should take the direct route at full speed; or they should pursue a zig-zag course at the highest possible speed. He favoured the zig-zag alternative.

Captain Petersen at once raised objections, partly because he thought the U-boat officer was upstaging him, and after all he was the Captain. A liner as big as the *Gustloff* could not swerve about all over the ocean, he argued.

In that case, declared the irate submarine officer, who knew more about the dangers of U-boat attack than any other person on board, they must make a run for it and go full ahead. He demanded a speed of sixteen knots.

Theoretically the Commander was right. It was perfectly

possible for a large and fast ocean liner to outpace the slow moving U-boats of the time and escape their attentions without benefit of an escort. The British had safely sailed the *Queen Mary* across the Atlantic in this style, greatly to the irritation of German U-boat commanders.

But the old Captain, who knew his ship well, sneered at Zahn. Despite popular belief, the *Gustloff* was not a really fast ship even in her heyday. She had not been built to compete for the Blue Riband but as an economically-run single-class ship to make National Socialist propaganda. Sixteen knots had been her top speed in ideal conditions with good maintenance and an experienced crew.

Petersen argued that if they tried for sixteen knots they would have red-hot bearings in five minutes. He pointed out that she had suffered bomb damage and the propeller casing had never been satisfactorily repaired. He insisted that in normal conditions he would never have taken the ship to sea at all in such a state. Twelve knots, he said, was the absolute maximum.

By this time the old man was thoroughly upset and Commander Zahn, though angry and frustrated, could do nothing about his decision. The weather was getting worse and the ratings sent out on deck to try to clear ice from the 30 mm light anti-aircraft guns returned numb with cold. It seemed a pointless exercise, for in the storm, the snow and the black night, the crews would not have been able to see aircraft anyway. "God help us all," said Zahn.

Below decks things seemed just as bad among the refugees, who by this time had got over their elation at managing to escape on a comfortable ship and were now subject to all the discomforts of a crowded vessel in bad weather. The lavatories were blocked and stinking. The women auxiliaries in their swimming pool quarters were sick; and because the ventilation was inadequate to cope with the quantity of breathing humanity aboard, it became insufferably hot. People began taking off their lifejackets and then their coats and pullovers.

Ruth Fleischer, the young wife of a naval officer, attracted attention among her fellow passengers because she insisted on obeying her husband's final instructions to keep on her lifebelt and warm clothes at all costs. Other passengers tried to persuade her to make herself more comfortable.

At about 2000 hours when the watches were relieved and frozen look-outs made their way below to thaw out in the warmth of the engine room messes, the bridge received another signal. As they ploughed their way along parallel to the Pomeranian coast they were fast approaching a group of minesweepers on a counter-course. There was danger of collision in the black and stormy night.

After a hasty consultation, Commander Zahn recommended that green and red navigation lights should be switched on to avoid the risk of collision with friendly vessels. So far as the officers knew the minesweepers were the only ships anywhere near. The only other ships to be expected in this stretch of sea were the heavy cruiser *Admiral Hipper* and her escort the T 36, a new 600-ton torpedo boat which had left the Gulf of Danzig several hours behind the *Gustloff*. They were due to overtake the *Gustloff* on a parallel course about midnight.

The *Hipper* was being pulled out of the fight. She was no longer capable of operations with the 2nd Battle Group because of the effects of damage sustained in an action with British ships in 1942 and because of a shortage of crew; and also because her oil reserves had been commandeered to keep the convoys running. The shortage of fuel was a constant problem for naval command. The decision had therefore been taken to move the *Hipper* out of the East Baltic where she was becoming vulnerable. Now she was on her way to Kiel with 1,377 refugees on board. Her escort, the T 36 which, under Lieutenant Commander Robert Hering, was to play a notable part in the unfolding drama, carried 250 refugees.

The fact that these two powerful warships would be in the same sea area as the fleeing liner in the middle of the night had indeed influenced Submarine Command when they ordered the *Gustloff* to sail alone.

It was a reassuring thought also to the worried staff of the Escort Division that the *Hipper*, even if she did not slow down and accompany the *Gustloff*, would at least be sailing within reasonable distance of the liner for two or three critical hours in the middle of the night. In those waters at that time German ships were badly in need of friends with firepower.

So, loaded down with her miserable cargo, with quarrelling officers on the bridge, with her speed reduced by engine problems, with navigation lights on in defiance of all normal wartime practice, and escorted by just one small vessel, the former pride of the Strength Through Joy movement sailed to her fate.

14

SOVIET NAVAL HEADQUARTERS in Kronstadt had no idea where Marinesko and the S 13 had got to. They had not heard from him for forty-eight hours. But Captain L. A. Kurnikov, the chief of staff, was not worried about his wayward ace. He knew that Marinesko hated using his radio transmitter.

After the war Marinesko wrote an account of his actions in the literary journal *Zvezda*. He recalled: "We were prowling up and down outside the Fascist lair but the dogs wouldn't come out and fight. I decided that the next day I would take the war to them, get a fix on the Hela lighthouse and sneak into Danzig Bay itself. There was danger from mines, but if the Nazi ships were able to get out it meant that the S 13 would be able to get in. It was a chance worth taking."

For the moment, however, everything aboard S 13 was boringly normal for a long-distance patrol. The boat was stuffy, smelly with sweat and engine oil. The big attack telescope rose from its well with a hiss of hydraulic rods as Marinesko scanned the sea.

When silent running was ordered voices were muted, those men not on duty lay in their bunks, and the loudest noise came from the running of the electric motors and quiet orders from the Captain to the men at the boat's controls. Once they sighted a single ship zig-zagging westwards at high speed but it was already too far away for them to give chase. There had been trawlers and other small boats battling through increasingly rough seas. Marinesko had rejected them. In the submariners' phrase they were "*myelochi*" ("small change"). There had, however, been one frightening experience. They had been passed at close range by another submarine. The sound of its propellers was heard clearly in the S 13 and the hydrophones had picked up the clicks of the electric switches altering speed on the other boat's motors. It passed by so close that its wake rocked the S 13, while the sound of its propellers gradually faded as it went about its business.

The man in charge of the hydrophones was Petty Officer Ivan Schnaptsev. Slimly built and twenty-three years old, he was naturally enough known to the crew as "Big Ears" because of the earphones he wore as he listened for victims – or attackers. At nightfall on January 30th he pronounced the seas clear and Marinesko took the S 13 to the surface and climbed through the hatch on to the conning tower. The regulation dress for submarine officers was a "*ushanka*" (a navy blue fur cap bearing a naval badge), sea boots, uniform trousers and a padded protective coat which was common to all services. Marinesko, however, favoured a grimy sheepskin overcoat, and he needed it that night. For as he, Yefremenkov and two look-outs emerged into the air, they were hit by a bitterly cold wind, lashing them and the S 13 with snow and freezing spray. The thermometer showed a temperature of minus seventeen degrees centigrade.

The navigator, Redkoborodov, writing in a Leningrad newspaper in 1970, remembered the atmosphere on board when they surfaced: "We had been on patrol for twenty days and we hadn't fired a shot in anger. But we now sensed we were where we should have been all the time. We knew that one way or another our luck was about to change. Either we got something or something got us. We were tensed up and ready for action."

But for the moment all was routine. Down below, as the fans began to drive fresh air through the boat and the diesels took over while the batteries were recharging, the crew were wondering who would be lucky enough to get up top for a smoke. On the conning tower with Marinesko and Yefremenkov was Petty Officer Anatoli Vinogradov, a swarthy Muscovite. He was forward look-out but he had already put aside his binoculars which were made useless by the spray and snow. The aft look-out was Petty Officer Andrei Pikhur, the boat's twenty-eight-year-old torpedo expert who had won the Order of Lenin for his marksmanship during the S 13's successful patrol the previous October. According to the account of Victor Germanov, a Soviet journalist, Marinesko remained on the conning tower while he made sure that there were no anti-submarine boats waiting to ram and depth charge him, set the surface routine going and then said to Yefremenkov: "I'm going below for a hot drink. Keep your eyes open, the bastards are out there somewhere. They've got to be."

He had no qualms about handing over to Yefremenkov. They had sailed together for nearly three years. Tall, saturnine, with a deadpan expression, Yefremenkov was the perfect counterpart to the swashbuckling Marinesko. The Captain's place on the conning tower was taken by a junior telegraphist who later remembered that he badly needed a smoke but his "*papirosa*" cigarette was destroyed by the wind and he had thrown the wet hollow cardboard tip over the side and cursed the weather.

It was at that moment that Vinogradov, pointing in the direction of the coastline, picked out some lights. At first they thought it was one of the lighthouses which gave warning of the Hela spit. Yefremenkov had studied the charts before they surfaced and he thought it likely that the lights came from the Rixhöft lighthouse on the coast itself, just to the west of the point where Hela joined the mainland. But it was possible that it might be the Heisternest light halfway along Hela.

He called Redkoborodov to the conning tower to get an accurate fix on their position. But the fact that the lights were on meant more than just an opportunity to establish their position – in fact they never did manage to do that correctly, for the coordinates which Marinesko later gave for the action were some ten miles out – but the very fact that the Germans had risked switching them on meant that a convoy was on the move out of the Bay of Danzig and would soon be rounding Hela to run for safety to the west.

This was confirmed when Vinogradov reported more lights. Now it was clear they *were* ships. Yefremenkov called Marinesko back to the bridge and sounded the alarm ordering the crew to action stations. It was 2110 hours (Russian time).

Marinesko's first decision was to reduce the S 13's buoyancy so that she rode lower in the water, presenting a much smaller silhouette to the enemy's look-outs and radar. The waves breaking over the boat would also help to confuse radar operators who would find it difficult to pick out the submarine against the "clutter" caused by the waves.

The S 13 took on the appearance of a rock at half tide over which the sea breaks and then draws back. It posed a delicate problem for the helmsman, Nikolai Toropov. If he lost control then the submarine could dip under the waves with its officers still on the bridge and with the hatch open. If that happened she would dive to the bottom of the sea – and stay there.

Schnaptsev was hard at work with his hydrophones. He reported: "Propeller bearings 160. Going away fast. One big vessel with twin screws. Possibly a cruiser." It was a report which must have pleased Marinesko, for no Soviet submarine in the war had yet sunk any warship larger than a minesweeper. It was also a good guess. Cruisers had in fact been standing offshore and giving fire support to the German Army, and a few hours later the *Admiral Hipper* was due to pass this spot on its way out of the battle.

Redkoborodov plotted an interception course and then, according to Germanov's somewhat highly coloured account, Marinesko "growled to Yefremenkov: 'I think we had better push her along a bit. We don't want to be late for our rendezvous. The sons of bitches would never forgive us.'"

Whether or not he used these exact words, they are in keeping with his character. We also know that behind his rebellious, hard-man manner, he was a thoughtful student of underwater warfare who had formed the view that Soviet

Admiral Doenitz, who masterminded Germany's "Dunkirk," the evacuation to the West of two million Germans from the Eastern Provinces

Above: An ecstatic crowd gives the Nazi salute as the *Wilhelm Gustloff* is launched, watched by Hitler and the Nazi hierarchy from a dais on the right of the picture.

Opposite: Souvenir postcards show one of the spacious promenade decks and the saloon.

The *Wilhelm Gustloff* in peacetime as a "Strength Through Joy" cruise liner

Frau Paula Knust, a German Naval Auxiliary

Frau Knust's boarding pass and the official form
certifying her rescue by TS 2

Above: War artist Professor Bock in his cabin

Opposite, above: A rare shot of the S13, said to have been taken while loading torpedoes at the Finnish port of Hangö, at the start of the January 1944 patrol

Opposite, below: Gauleiter Erich Koch, the man responsible for hundreds and thousands of deaths in Poland and the Ukraine

Captain Alexander Marinesko of the S 13 and (*below*) his navigator, Captain Lieutenant Nikolai Redkoborodov

tactics would have to change fundamentally if the submarines were to sink the escaping convoys.

What he had long wanted to try was the German method – attacking on the surface and using the S 13 as a submersible torpedo boat rather than as a submarine, a daring manoeuvre directly opposed to conservative Russian and British teaching. At first it brought the Germans astounding success. It was best for a nighttime attack with the submarine penetrating the screen of escort vessels and getting into the convoy lanes on the dark side of the ships, preferably with a helpful moon silhouetting the targets. On the surface the submarine could run and manoeuvre almost as fast as the escort vessels and all its armament could be brought into use. It was able to fire its torpedoes with greater accuracy and, cruising inside the convoy lanes, caused chaos among the merchant ships and brought frustration to the escort.

It was also, of course, highly dangerous, and long-range aircraft fitted with radar which pinpointed the U-boats on the surface at night eventually led to so many sinkings that the vessels went undersea again. The radar aircraft would pick up the U-boat on its scanner and then, when in range, would switch on its Leigh Light, a powerful searchlight, and the submarine would become a sitting target.

But these developments did not worry Marinesko because the Germans had no airborne anti-submarine radar in the Baltic. All he had to worry about was the escort vessels, and the Germans were desperately short of these. He considered that if the approach was carried out carefully it could be done without too much risk. And Marinesko, however undisciplined he was ashore, was a very careful man at sea. He decided to attack on the surface.

15

OFTEN IN THE Baltic winter the wind hustles snowstorms off the land. They arrive without warning, make a ship blind and are gone as suddenly as they appear. Just such a storm blanketed the S 13. Nothing could be seen from the conning tower. The lights had vanished. And then, as the snow whirled away, Marinesko was able to see not only lights but the shapes of two ships, one small and the other very large.

In a conversation quoted in the official history of the Baltic Fleet, Marinesko recalled:

> When the snow cleared suddenly I saw the silhouette of an ocean liner. It was enormous. It even had some lights showing. There and then I decided it was about 20,000 tons, certainly not less. And I was sure it was packed with men who had trampled on Mother Russia and were now fleeing for their lives. It had to be sunk, I decided, and the S 13 would do the job. It was now only a question of where and when. I had already mentally prepared for the surface attack in order to increase the probability of hitting the target with a bow volley.
>
> And then it came to me that I would have to sweep round the back of the convoy and attack it from the shore. They would not expect an attack from that direction. Their watch would be concentrating on looking out to sea. All we had to do was to get our calculations right and not panic. We would worry about the minesweeper later.

He ran the S 13 at full speed until it was positioned on a parallel course to the *Wilhelm Gustloff* between the ship and the coast. They were now down-moon and were in danger of being seen when the moon emerged from the cloud and snow flurries. In compensation, the coastline provided a dark background. It was a question of luck – and how good a watch the Germans kept.

There were two anxious moments. A flare suddenly climbed above the horizon, hung for a while and then faded out. Marinesko wondered if he had been spotted or if the flare indicated a change of course. Then the liner began signalling by lamp in what appeared to be the S 13's direction. Vinogradov, who knew some German and had studied German naval recognition signals, flashed back a brief reply which he hoped made sense. Nothing happened.

Marinesko hugged the coastline with the liner and the minesweeper to starboard at a distance of some 2,000 metres. His two main fears were of being caught in a minefield or of being spotted and having to crash dive in only thirty metres of water. In either case the S 13 would be extremely lucky to survive. On the conning tower preparations were made for the attack. Redkoborodov sang out the key details: "Target's course 280 degrees. Speed 15 knots. Distance 12 cables." The nightsight had been fitted to the master sight and the covers removed from the torpedo firing switches. Captain Lieutenant Vladimir Krylov, the political officer, went among the crew telling them what was going on.

It had taken the S 13 nearly two hours to overtake the *Gustloff* and Marinesko found it incredible that he had remained undetected for such a long time on the surface. It would not have been possible if there had been a strong escort. He could not understand why the big ship was not zig-zagging and why she was showing lights. He ordered the S 13 to turn towards its target.

The *Löwe*, the forlorn escort of the *Wilhelm Gustloff*, battered her way through heavy seas ahead of the liner. They had already passed Rixhöft, and were coming up to the shallows of the Stolpe Bank which they would pass on their port side, forcing them out into deeper water. Although he had no means of knowing it, Marinesko had little to worry about from the *Löwe*, for she was completely blind; her submarine detection gear was out of action. It had frozen solid and apart from her look-outs she no longer had any way of detecting enemy vessels.

But on the *Gustloff*, for the first time, all seemed to be going well. The passengers had settled down despite their seasickness and the ship was making good progress. A few more hours should see them out of danger. Captain Petersen could see the reassuring white stern light of the *Löwe* through the bridge window. There was no sign, no hint of trouble. Together with Commander Zahn and Louis Reese he went to the first officer's cabin for their first meal since sailing. The head steward, Max Bonnet, correctly dressed in his white jacket, served them pea soup and a plate of cold meat. With food inside them the officers began to relax after the troubles and quarrels of the previous twenty-four hours. At the end of the meal Zahn ordered cognac for the three of them to drink a toast to a good trip.

At the navigation table the third officer was busy taking a fix on the ship's position from the flashing lights of the Rixhöft and Stilo lighthouses. Captain Weller, who was officer of the watch, told him to take over while he went to the chart room to check the position and make sure they were on course. He checked the time. It was 2104 hours (German time).

The S 13 closed in from the port side. Yefremenkov set the nightsight. The four bow torpedo tubes were cleared for surface firing and Marinesko ordered the torpedoes to be set to run at a depth of three metres. He checked the time. It was 2304 hours (Russian time).

Redkoborodov chanted the range course and bearing. The target was under a thousand metres away and loomed large in Yefremenkov's nightsight. He waited for the liner's bow to touch the intersection of the illuminated crosswires. They touched and Marinesko gave the order to fire.

Before the S 13 had left Hangö, Petty Officer Pikhur

painted slogans on the torpedoes. They were predictable, politically safe and had an order about them which would have pleased Krylov, the political officer. In Tube One the torpedo carried the slogan: "For the Motherland." In Tube Two: "For Stalin." In Tube Three: "For the Soviet People" and in Tube Four: "For Leningrad."

The torpedoes from Tubes One, Three and Four ran true. They struck home in a burst of orange flame. The explosions sounded in the submarine like blows on a slack drumskin. But the torpedo from Tube Two, "For Stalin", hung in its tube – primed ready to blow the submarine and everyone in her to pieces at the slightest impact.

The S 13's log reads: "23.08. Three bow torpedoes fired at target's port side. All hit. Distance 2.5 to 3 cables. 23.09 Target began to sink."

16

WELLER WAS JUST going through the door to return to his place on the bridge when there was a loud, dull explosion which lifted him so that his head hit the top of the door. "Mines," he shouted and rushed to the engine telegraph to ring "Stop". There were two more explosions. Then alarm bells started to sound.

Just aft, in the first officer's cabin, glasses and plates crashed to the floor and Commander Zahn's Alsatian, Hassan, who had been lying on the bunk, let out a howl and leapt to the floor. The three officers ran down the now tilting deck. The ship's head was already down and she was listing five degrees.

Commander Zahn, the experienced submariner, knew that the *Gustloff* had been hit by three torpedoes. Captain Weller was trying to get through to the engine room, but both the telephone and the public address systems were dead. The explosions had already stopped the engines. The officers on the bridge could hear noises from below which indicated that some bulkheads had gone.

Walter Knust, the second engineer officer, was asleep in the engine room while waiting to go on watch. He had chosen to wait below so as not to disturb his wife, Paula Maria, in their cabin. To make himself more comfortable he had taken off his shoes and socks and jacket.

"I heard two loud explosions and I knew what had happened at once, because the engines stopped and then I saw a rush of water through the engine room. First the ship lurched to starboard under the force of the blast. Then she rose and began listing to port. I put on my shoes and jacket and hurried out into the corridor."

Up in the radio room Rudi Lange was struggling with his

equipment. The ship's main radio was out of action, and the emergency sets were not functioning properly.

"I grabbed an army transmitter which had been brought on board for emergencies, and with freezing hands began sending out the SOS signal," Lange recalled later. *"Wilhelm Gustloff* sinking. Position – 55 degrees 07 North; 17 degrees 42 East. Please help."

But Lange's reserve transmitter had a range of only 2,000 metres, and the message could not be picked up back at naval headquarters. The *Löwe*, steaming ahead of the liner, had not noticed that the ship she was escorting was no longer under way. It was not until her radio operator picked up Lange's faint distress signal that her Captain knew that the *Wilhelm Gustloff* was in trouble.

As the *Löwe* began to go about to return to the stricken liner her more powerful radio began re-transmitting the SOS. But the message was not put out on the frequency reserved for warships of the 9th Escort Division. It went out over the emergency frequency for the U-boat Division convoy, and for this reason the first news of the drama aboard the *Gustloff* was heard by the radio officer of the *Hansa*. Thus valuable time was lost in alerting rescue forces at a time when the *Gustloff* was only some twenty-five miles offshore and within short sailing time of a number of German ships.

Commander Heydel told the authors: "The mistake was that at our headquarters in Swinemunde we did not hear anything about the movement of the *Wilhelm Gustloff* until after the disaster had happened, yet she was supposed to be in our area."

The war diary of the neighbouring 10th Escort Division contains this entry:

At 23.00 received following radio message: Square 9452. Ship sinking fast. MII8.

MII8 not known here. Hence not yet verifiable which ship is meant. Only messages arriving at about 23.30

clearly indicate that the *Wilhelm Gustloff* sank at about 22.18 at 55 degrees 7.5 North and 17 degrees 42 East. Causes as yet unknown.

Only now received telex Strength Through Joy G93 of 30 January that *Wilhelm Gustloff* passed the Hela coast-guard at 15.15 with the escorting torpedo boat *Löwe*, so the Escort Division knew of the sinking of the ship before it heard about her departure and presence within our own area . . . Signed *Leiter Chef* (Chief Leader) Second Escort Flotilla.

Opposite the radio cabin was the one occupied by Professor Bock. He had gone there together with Baroness von Maydell after a comfortable dinner of cold beef and a bottle of burgundy served under the supervision of the ubiquitous Max Bonnet, who was emerging as the Jeeves of the *Wilhelm Gustloff*. After dinner Gunther von Maydell went down to the cabin he shared with his mother and another woman and her daughter on the upper Promenade Deck. Professor Bock had just opened a bottle of wine and Baroness von Maydell was reading a little romantic verse when they felt the first explosion. It sent books and glasses crashing to the cabin floor. The first thought of the Baroness was for her son.

"I hurried down the corridor to go and find him. By this time there were dim emergency lights. People were rushing about and screaming. Alarm bells shrilled. It was such a relief when I saw Gunther coming up to look for me, and then the Professor led the way up to the Boat Deck."

When the torpedoes struck, Gunther had been lying on his bunk reading an Indian adventure story by Karl May, the German childrens' author. Cabin 40 was a comfortable one which still had all the hallmarks of a pre-war cruise liner. There were books in the shelves and crystal flasks on his mother's dressing table. "I am glad we are at sea at last," he had said to his mother just before she left the cabin. Gunther von Maydell still remembers the moment when the torpedoes struck – "Vroom – Vroom – Vroom! That's what it sounded like."

For a thirteen-year-old he was remarkably collected. It was the other woman in the cabin who was in a panic. "What shall we do?" she cried. Gunther told her to put on a coat and a lifebelt, and she rushed off to find her daughter who had gone to another cabin with some friends. The boy, who had got to know the topography of the ship, then went off in search of his mother.

"Once we had found Gunther, I ran back with him to my cabin to get coats, and also my gloves and hat, for it was bitterly cold," recounted Professor Bock. "I remember thinking that it would be mad to leave my fur coat behind if the ship was sinking. Then I led them all to the starboard side of the Boat Deck. Already we were listing heavily to port and I knew it would be difficult to get the boats away."

They ran up the frozen and sloping deck to one of the lifeboats where sailors were already trying to operate the winches. It was an almost impossible task, for the machinery was frozen stiff and the scratch crew was ill-trained to get lifeboats away smoothly in such conditions.

The privileged passengers with cabins of their own, even crowded ones, were the most fortunate, for at least they were on the upper decks within easy reach of the open air and the boats. For the mass of refugees packed into the public rooms on the lower decks things were more desperate. Few of them knew anything about the layout of the ship, and hardly any had bothered to look for the emergency exits which had been carefully signposted by the crew before sailing. They had been glad just to get passage on an escape ship, and for the many who had never before been to sea there was no means of knowing how to get out.

On E and D Decks, they were battered by the blast which swept along the narrow companionways. For a while the interior was in darkness until the emergency lighting went on, and the whole place reeked of fumes from the explosion.

Stumbling along blindly, the refugees thought they would have to find the place where they had entered the ship, and there were few crew members to direct them. The passageways soon filled with panic-stricken women and children.

Second Engineer Knust, hurrying to his wife's cabin from the engine room, reported that he found the passageways already crowded. "I saw a lot of people being seasick. I told them to follow me because I knew a way out, but they did not seem to want to. I just hope they were able to die peacefully."

The first torpedo hit the *Gustloff* forward on the port side, a few metres below the waterline. But on the Bridge at that time they had no detailed information about the extent of the damage, for none of the crew had been able to get there to check. There was no communication between the bridge and the positions below decks where damage control squads should have been on duty.

Captain Weller tried to make sure that damage control parties closed the watertight bulkheads, and sealed off areas near the blasted hull. And, on their own initiative, *Gustloff* seamen did succeed in closing some. But it was a grim decision to make and equally grim to carry out, for to close the bulkheads was to condemn to death anyone on the wrong side of them.

The forward torpedo had struck the forecastle hard by the crew's quarters, and most of those off duty perished in flying metal and the first onrush of water. Those who survived, still dazed with blast and the stench of explosive gases, were now trapped behind those bulkheads which were sealed off to prevent the ship sinking immediately. The seamen drowning in the forward compartments were the men who should have been helping passengers to the Boat Deck, and who should have manned the lifeboats. And there was nobody to replace them, for even the U-boat sailors were not properly trained for such duties.

The second torpedo exploded just under the E Deck swimming pool where the Naval Auxiliary girls had been billeted.

All that remained there now were bodies, smashed metal, woodwork, and fragments of the "classical" murals which had decorated the pool and its surroundings.

The third torpedo hit the forward part of the engine room amidships, tearing open the hull and destroying the engines.

A few of the navy girls survived the explosions. They had been packed into cabins between the swimming pool and the engine room, because there was not enough room for them all in the drained pool area. Among them was Gertrud Agnesons, a seventeen-year-old who had been put into a cabin with five other members of her section.

The explosion woke Gertrud in her stuffy little cabin. In the darkness she was unable to move. Her ears were still ringing with the noise when she heard one of the other girls shout hysterically: "Air alarm, air alarm."

After several seconds she jumped down from her bunk and tried to put the light on. Somebody else jumped on top of her. "I've lost the key to the cupboard. My lifejacket is there," shrieked a third girl.

She lit a match and burnt her finger as she and the others scrabbled for the key in ankle-deep water. Then they lit another match and tried to break down the door which was jammed tight shut.

Suddenly a jet of water "thick as a man's arm" poured on to them from above, putting out the match. By the light of another they saw a girl lying on her bunk, whimpering, and unable to move. She had a torch but was incapable of making the effort to switch it on. There was a mad expression on her face, so Gertrud grabbed the torch.

By its light they managed to open the door and force their way into the gangway. Gertrud tried to run through water already up to her thighs, and she saw with horror the body of a dead girl floating past and then some sandwiches drifting on the surface. She vaguely remembered having noticed an emergency exit sign and she made for it. Nobody bothered to follow her, for the other girls were all heading for the main staircase, and by the time Gertrud reached the first rung of an iron ladder up the ship's side she was alone.

She scrambled up it to the next deck and found herself in an empty corridor. All the cabin doors were swinging open but there was nobody in sight. Completely lost, she ran along the deck. Then a sailor appeared and she shouted at him: "Wait! Help! I can't get out."

The dazed sailor did not seem to understand. "Have you seen my girlfriend?" he asked. "She was in the swimming pool. Where is she?"

He began going down the iron ladder. In a panic Gertrud again screamed: "Help. Where is the way out?"

"You must be blind," he said. "Just through there to the right."

Gertrud Agnesons pushed her way through a door and found herself borne along by the pushing, screaming and fighting crowd on the stairway.

There was only one thought in every mind among the panic-stricken thousands, and that was to climb upwards towards the open decks and a chance to escape the inrushing sea. As they climbed, with Gertrud Agnesons now among them, they pushed against each other remorselessly. Anyone who fell was trampled underfoot in the great scrum. Small children who slipped from their mothers' arms were trodden to death.

Another of the girl sailors, nineteen-year-old Sigrid Bergfeld, squeezed through a gap blasted in the wall of a cabin. Up to her waist in water, she fought her way along a companionway before she found an iron ladder which led her to the main stairway and eventually to the Boat Deck.

Those strong and fortunate enough to reach the places where main staircases opened on to the Boat Deck found themselves penned in by the narrow doors leading on to it. There were desperate scenes as they tried to force a way out.

On the Sun Deck Lieutenant Dankel, one of the ship's officers, mustered a party of two or three ratings on the starboard side to try to stem the rush and impose some sort of order as those who broke through began to storm the boats.

He gave that traditional order: "Women and children first." But few listened to him. The men were stronger and it was they who were pushing hardest. Within twenty minutes there was total panic even though the communication system had been repaired and the bridge was broadcasting messages of reassurance. Lieutenant Dankel and other officers trying to hold back the advancing tide of people shouted in vain that there was room for all aboard the lifeboats. That might have been true if everybody had remained calm, but few did.

In exasperation Dankel drew his pistol and fired warning shots. He became even angrier when one of the sailors reported: "Herr Lieutenant: some of the crew have taken a lifeboat for themselves."

He opened fire again as the lifeboat with room for fifty people hit the sea with only a dozen *Gustloff* sailors in it.

"Swine," he cried and fired again. But there was nothing he could do. More and more people surged on to the deck, and his own deck party watched helplessly as the crew in their lifeboat, having failed to get its engine started, took to the oars and rowed away from the side of the ship.

Number four lifeboat was the first one to get away properly. It, too, had a number of crew members on board, but at least they tried to get women and children into the boat before lowering it away. Because order had completely broken down, hundreds of people who could have been saved perished in the ugly fight for life on the Boat Deck.

Sigrid Bergfeld, after a determined struggle, found herself at one of the few lifeboat stations where something like order prevailed. A sailor pushed her forward and told her to get in. But, just at that moment, she was jostled by a woman carrying a baby, and she held back for a second. The woman got in, and they began lowering the boat away. Sigrid watched the boat go down, and then capsize as it hit the waves, throwing all its passengers into the sea.

Pushing through the crowd, she moved too late towards another lifeboat. That one too was badly launched by men acting hastily and without coordination. Hanging by its forward line this boat spilled its screaming passengers into the sea. Then a few moments later the line snapped and the heavy boat fell on top of those still struggling in the water.

There was nobody at hand to help the most unfortunate of all the passengers on board, the pregnant women and the badly-wounded and limbless soldiers in the emergency hospital in the "Arbour", just forward of the bridge superstructure – the place where, in peacetime, the cruise passengers had taken their leisurely drinks and watched through the big glass window as the sunlit sea slid by.

In the early stages a doctor and a few orderlies managed to carry out some of these helpless men and women on to the Boat Deck. But they were unable to fend for themselves and had no means of getting into the boats. Petty Officer Schottes found a number of sailors skulking in a lifeboat and managed to bully them out of it to help the wounded soldiers to a boat. But there were few people ready to give such assistance.

By this time the port side was well down in the water and this made the launching of boats difficult. But on the starboard side, increasingly high out of the water with the exposed metalwork of the ship's side sticking out like the ridge of a pyramid, the situation was even worse.

There are no surviving witnesses of the most dreadful scenes of all. In the crew's section where the first torpedo exploded, nearly a quarter of the Merchant Navy deck-hands – all those off duty – were trapped on the wrong side of the steel watertight doors. These were now inexorably closed, for otherwise the water, rushing in through the huge hole opened up by the torpedo in the ship's side, would have cascaded on and swamped the rest of the ship. For the trapped men, therefore, there was no way out; they drowned as the water rose.

In other parts of the ship refugees were trapped in the same fashion. And witnesses among those fighting their way to other decks reported hearing the crack of pistol shots from the other side of the watertight doors. It seems only too likely that anyone with a firearm in those parts of the ship would have preferred to shoot himself and his loved ones rather than wait for a slower and more horrifying death by water.

Heinz Schoen, who interviewed survivors during the 1950s, reported one such incident in a lower deck cabin. A sailor ran down one corridor forcing open jammed doors. He heard a shot in one of the cabins and broke down the door. On the floor lay the bodies of a woman and a small child. In the centre of the cabin was a naval officer holding a still smoking pistol while a terrified five-year-old boy clutched his father's leg. "Get out!" ordered the officer, staring vacantly at the sailor. And there was no doubt in the mind of the sailor that he had intruded on a family suicide pact.

The same source reported a similar incident concerning a high Nazi Party official on board. A sailor named Dorch, trying desperately not to slip from the icy deck, heard the official's wife a few yards away shout at her husband: "Put a quick end to us all!" There were three shots as the man killed his wife and two children, then silence when his weapon jammed as he tried to end his own life. He shouted to Dorch to borrow his pistol but then lost his balance and fell into the sea.

17

WHILE SOME CHOSE suicide, thousands were clinging to the hope that they might be rescued. Armed sailors had sealed off the glass windowed area of the Upper Promenade Deck some 170 metres long. By threatening to shoot anyone who broke out they had herded together hundreds of passengers who had fought their way to the upper decks. Loud-hailer messages constantly assured the passengers that if they waited calmly they would soon be rescued. Nevertheless, the sailors had to use their weapons to hold in those who were not convinced by these assurances.

Engineer Officer Walter Knust was able to escape from the engine room. After two years in the *Gustloff*, he knew every passageway. He ran to his cabin, knocked down the door and brought out his wife. Outside, the gangway was packed with screaming people making for the main exits.

"I grabbed my wife by her blazer, so as not to lose her in the crowd," Knust told the authors. "I knew at once that the only hope of getting through this mob to the Boat Deck was to make for the iron ladder up the side used by the crew, and I shouted to others to follow, but they took no notice.

"When we got to the Boat Deck it was swarming with passengers. I saw people jumping over the side; some of them even took off their clothes before they plunged into the water, and they must have died at once of the cold. I shouted to people to put on all their clothes, but they were too shocked to do what I told them."

Frau Knust, now divorced from the former second engineer and re-married, vividly remembered the scene as they got to the upper deck. "We struggled through the crowd to one of the boats. It was so cold as the wind hit us. I was wearing only slacks and a blouse and blazer. Already the ship had a heavy list. The waves seemed very high, and you cannot imagine how terrible it looked.''

Knust, as a ship's officer, had been detailed to take charge of one of the boats in an emergency. It was not a regular lifeboat, but a small motor pinnace installed in the liner's cruising days for use when she was in the Norwegian fjords.

''I told my wife to hang on to the rail while I got to work on the frozen fastenings,'' he told the authors. ''It was really hard work because everything was blocked with snow and ice. Until you are in an emergency you just do not know what you can do, and with my bare hands I managed to get the boat free.

''I was alone working on my boat and the job was not made any easier by the increasing list to port. I had managed to get it free but even when I had loosened the lashings I just could not get it to swing out.

''I paused and pushed my wife up into the boat. Then a woman with a three-week-old baby appeared and I got her in as well.

''A man called Roger, a leading electrician, came up and gave me a hand to push and shove.

''While we were trying to swing the stern of the boat over the side the crew of the next boat, who saw we were having trouble, shouted to us to get into theirs. But this one was my responsibility and I stayed with it. The man who had shouted slipped on the icy deck as she swung away and fell overboard. He broke his back when he hit the rail of the deck below and died immediately.

''Once we managed to get our boat outboard I slid in down a rope and she was lowered away on the electric winches. As she passed the lower decks women trapped on the Promenade Deck shouted to us to stop and pick them up. There was nothing we could do.

''My main worry was how to unhitch the hooks fastening the boat to the lowering lines, because we had no crew. But luckily after we landed on the water a wave hit us and that freed us from the lines. Then I remember thinking, 'We still have to get away from the side of the ship otherwise it may fall on top of us.' I began pushing us away from the ship's side with one of the oars."

The same anxiety was in the mind of his wife, who recalls thinking that their boat would be swamped by the sinking liner. "As we hit the water I could see people leaping from the side of the ship into the sea. I thought those who escaped drowning would freeze to death. It was so cold."

Among those who did leap into the sea at this stage, according to Schoen, was the ship's barber who had taken such care to collect silver five Deutschmark pieces. Before fighting his way up on deck he had collected his rucksack full of coins and strapped it on his back. He jumped with the idea of landing in a boat, but missed and was borne down under the waves by the weight of his hoarded coins. He was never seen again.

After the initial alarm caused by the explosion and the heavy list of the ship, the passengers who survived the blast grew calmer as hope rekindled that they might be rescued. Captains Weller and Kohler on the Bridge had sent down deck parties to assess the damage. They fired distress signals. The ship began to stabilise and for a while there was hope that she might settle by the stern on the sea bottom long enough for rescue ships to arrive.

The Bridge continued to broadcast comforting messages: "The ship will not sink", and "Rescue ships are on their way, Kolberg is only a hundred miles away". These statements were made in hope rather than in the light of full information, but they gave much-needed reassurances.

As they waited anxiously by one of the lifeboats Professor Bock and his friends the von Maydells felt the ship lurch. Bock looked at his watch and saw that it was nine fifteen. Baroness von Maydell rushed forward and tried to get into the lifeboat they were still attempting to free.

"No," he shouted. "This is crazy. It just is not going to work. Follow me, I know where there is another boat."

He had watched the final preparations for sea at Gdynia and knew that the navy had brought cranes to lift naval cutters on to the Sun Deck behind the *Gustloff*'s funnel. They were simply lashed to the deck. It would be impossible to launch them, but at least there was a good chance that they might float away as the liner sank deeper into the water, for already waves were flowing over parts of the deck.

The deck was so angled and made so slippery by the combination of ice and water that they had to crawl on hands and knees along its treacherous surface. It took them nearly fifteen minutes to reach one of the cutters. There were not many people near it.

It was by now about nine-thirty and Ebbi von Maydell saw the purser, Gerhardt Luth, a big and well-built man, take off his lifejacket and strap it on to a woman waiting pitifully on the deck. He himself leapt overboard, and he was eventually picked up by one of the boats.

As they crawled they clutched at the sloping walls of the deckhousing. The ship kept shuddering and they were hard pressed to stay on the slippery deck.

"As it lurched I could see dozens of people sliding off into the sea. Just as we reached the boat deep water came pouring along the deck," said Ebbi von Maydell. "Gunther scrambled up into the boat and so did Professor Bock. Then he and a sailor reached over and pulled me up for I could not climb in by myself.

"Never in my life had I been treated so roughly. I thought they would break my neck, but I was just relieved to get in. It all happened in seconds. At that moment the ship seemed to be turning right over on her side."

18

Bock, exhausted by the effort of pulling people into the cutter, let go the high gunwale and dropped back into the boat. As he landed he almost hit a man crouching beneath, and with astonishment he saw four gold stripes glistening in the faint moonlight.

"My God, it's our Captain!" he exclaimed. It was indeed Captain Friedrich Petersen, master of the *Wilhelm Gustloff*. Both he and another *Gustloff* officer had installed themselves in this well-placed VIP lifeboat in the earlier panic.

Hardly were the Maydells and Bock into the cutter before a larger wave swept it in a frantic roller-coaster motion across the deck. It swung dizzily towards the funnel, and for a second they thought that the boat would be smashed against it. Next, the boat swirled towards the davits. They feared it would be caught on them, but the force of the swell finally flung it from ship's port side into the open sea.

Lieutenant Dankel, hanging on to the iron rung of a ladder on the funnel could see the cutters on the deck quite clearly. He could have got into one of them but from his higher position he could tell what danger they were in. He felt sure they would all end in disaster. He was amazed when the first cutter swung past and floated away safely from the ship. A second did the same but the third was hurled against deck fixtures and smashed to pieces.

About the same moment, Eva Luck, the sixteen-year-old refugee who had come aboard the *Gustloff* with her mother and six-year-old sister, was also swept off the deck. Fortunately she was wearing her lifejacket.

The Luck family had been trapped in the music room on

the Lower Promenade Deck with little hope of making a way out.

"Then suddenly the whole music room tilted and a great cry went up from all the people there," Eva later wrote in her diary. "They literally slid in a heap along the angled deck. A grand piano at one end went berserk and rolled across the crowded room crushing women and children in its path and scattering others before it. Finally it smashed into the port bulkhead with a discordant roar as though a giant fist had hit all the keys at once."

Eva picked up the suitcase with the family's silver in it and started to move, not in the least knowing how to escape. A sailor grabbed her by the arm: "Quick, you've got to get out," he shouted and led the little party through the mob.

"My mother had forgotten to put her shoes on, and I moved clumsily on high heels towards the iron rungs of the ladder going up the ship's inside. People around us were falling about as the ship moved but I was able to grasp the rungs and haul up my little sister, Dorrit. My mother followed us to the upper deck.

"When we got there it was terrible. I saw with horror that the funnel was lying almost parallel with the sea. People were jumping in. I could hear the ship's siren and felt the ice-cold water round my legs. I reached out to try and grab my sister. I felt nothing but the water as it swept me out and over the side."

The *Gustloff* shuddered as bulkheads and watertight doors gave way under the pressure of the thousands of tons of water swirling around the lower decks. In the end it took just sixty seconds for the great ship to fall over on to her port side bringing the funnel level with the water. Sailors working on the pumps were trapped and drowned. Only two managed to crawl out through an air vent.

Two thousand people were still imprisoned on the Lower Promenade Deck. Some had been marshalled there by armed sailors trying to restore order. Others, reassured by the

Bridge's optimistic bulletins and daunted by the cold and the horror of the open deck, had crept into shelter in the hope that help would soon arrive.

As the *Gustloff* listed until her decks were at right angles to the water, these passengers slid helplessly towards the windows which enclosed the deck. The glass shattered and they spilled out to their deaths. Only one person escaped from this area in the final minutes – Maria Kupfer, who scrambled on to the back of a man and climbed through a broken window on the starboard side which was now uppermost.

Heinz Schoen has terrible recollections of the moment when he found himself crawling across the frozen deck:

"You just cannot imagine what it was like," he told the authors in his smart house at Bad Saltzlufen where he keeps a library of *Wilhelm Gustloff* documentation. "For years afterwards I just could not bring myself to talk about it.

"It was dark. It was cold. When the first torpedo exploded I was sitting in my cabin on B Deck drinking cognac, feeling ill and exhausted after days of hard work. That is why I was drinking.

"The explosion threw me against the heating pipes. I knew that I had to get up and on the deck – and fast. I put on my uniform and coat and boots and started to move. But I can't quite explain. From then on everything seemed to happen in my subconscious. I was numb and dazed.

"I knew the way up, but I was so pushed and battered and jostled by the crowds that when I got there they had stripped most of my warm clothing from me. So at the end I was freezing cold, looking around for a way of escape. I saw a pile of square rafts stacked on the deck and clambered up into the top one.

"Sometimes I shouted up at people on the Bridge to ask how deep the water was on the tilting, heaving deck. I remember someone shouting ten metres. I just waited there knowing that there was absolutely nothing I could do. After what seemed like hours the raft just floated over the side and on to the sea. It was very simple and I was very lucky."

The only place where order prevailed in the final stages was on the Bridge. At 2150, forty-five minutes after the torpedoes had struck, with the wheelhouse indicator recording a list of twenty-five degrees and waves hitting the Bridge windows, Commander Zahn supervised the destruction of the ship's codes and papers. Then Steward Max Bonnet appeared, still wearing his white jacket. With enormous difficulty he managed to carry his tray. "A final cognac, gentlemen," he said. They drank and threw down the glasses.

For a few seconds the thick glass of the Bridge windscreen cleared and they caught a surrealistic glimpse of a couple of men climbing into a raft. Within seconds a huge wave seized the toylike craft and hurled it at the superstructure of the Bridge.

Zahn hung on to a rail and edged his way aft on the starboard side towards the remaining rafts. When he reached the empty davits of one of the lifeboats, he saw that a man had climbed on to one of the arms and was clinging to it. Not far away was a woman clutching a small child. "Please help," she screamed. But there was nothing anyone could do.

The woman threw her child up to the man on the davits. He reached for it with one hand, missed and the child fell to the deck and rolled into the sea. The wailing mother leapt after the baby.

Commander Zahn crawled on towards the only raft he could see. It was held by two ratings who shouted to him to give them a hand. Lying on his stomach he seized a short rope. Then a fresh wave hit the ship and hurled them all into the sea.

Thinking that he would be buried by the ship's final plunge, Zahn hit the water and went under. His lifejacket pulled him back to the surface and he saw a raft floating nearby as he struggled to fill his lungs with air.

He climbed up the short rope ladder, and from the raft could make out hundreds of heads bobbing up and down in the waves. He also noticed there were about twenty or thirty rafts close together and that all of them were empty. Anxious to get as far away from the wreck of the *Gustloff* as possible, he jumped from one raft to another until he fell exhausted into the fifth or sixth.

Behind him the *Gustloff* plunged, boiling and gurgling, into the shallow waters of the Baltic.

Every survivor watched with horror, for the end of the *Wilhelm Gustloff* seemed to anticipate in stagey melodrama the end of the Nazi régime itself. As she went under, her boiler room exploding, her generators and lighting system were re-activated.

From her lifeboat Ebbi von Maydell saw this extraordinary sight. "Suddenly it seemed that every light in the ship had come on. The whole ship was blazing with lights, and her sirens sounded out over the sea."

Frau Knust remembers watching from the boat where she sat, frozen, with her husband: "I cannot forget the loud clear sound of the siren as the *Gustloff* with all her lights on made the final plunge.

"I could clearly see the people still on board the *Gustloff* clinging to the rails. Even as she went under they were still hanging on and screaming. All around us were people swimming, or just floating in the sea. I can still see their hands grasping at the sides of our boat. It was too full to take on any more."

Walter Knust also paused to look as the liner's funnel finally hit the water. As it came parallel with the sea the ship started howling. It was horrible.

It had taken the *Wilhelm Gustloff* just over seventy minutes to sink; and now the ocean around her grave was dotted with figures fighting for their lives. Few of them lasted long. The cold, the waves, the dark, and the despair claimed all but the hardiest and the luckiest.

19

Marinesko kept the S 13 half submerged while he watched the *Wilhelm Gustloff* lurch and list. Once he was sure she was going to sink, and fearing that retribution would now be heading his way in the form of the liner's escort, he cleared the conning tower at speed and gave the command for the S 13 to be taken down to the doubtful safety of the shallow seabed. A sense of danger now pervaded the submarine. They waited for depth charges to fall about them. They knew that they had little room to manoeuvre, and they knew also that the "Stalin" torpedo was hung up in the Number Two tube, primed and ready to be set off by any shock. As the S 13 dived, the agony of the *Wilhelm Gustloff* could be heard through Schnaptsev's earphones: the bulkheads gave way with a groaning and grating as the pressure of thousands of tons of water broke them apart. But it was not to these doleful sounds that Schnaptsev's ears were principally attuned, but to the hint of pursuing propellers.

The danger in the torpedo tube was discovered by Vladimir Kurochkin, a burly, bearded, torpedo gunner's mate. He was renowned for his strength and the fluency of his curses. He told Germanov of his surprise when it dawned on him that only three torpedoes had left their tubes. . . . "So I gave the Number Two tube a bash. After all, I'm supposed to know how to make these things work. Nothing happened and it was then that the thought came to me that the whore was primed and its motor was running. And of course the tube was flooded and the propellers were beginning to turn and now I began to sweat because I knew that with the smallest burp the primer could start doing its job. Luckily a fault then developed in the compressed air vessel and the motor cut out."

He was then able to shut the outer doors of the torpedo tube and make it safe.

The S 13 was incredibly lucky. Because the *Gustloff* had only one escort, the *Löwe*, and because she was preoccupied with picking up survivors, it was some time before the depth charges started to come down, and by the time they did, "Stalin" had been made harmless.

20

FOUR HOURS AFTER the *Wilhelm Gustloff* sailed from Gdynia, the *Admiral Hipper* had weighed anchor, bound for Kiel. She was leaving the operational area of the Eastern Baltic and had taken on board military equipment, 1,377 refugees and 152 dockers.

Late in the afternoon she rendezvoused at sea with her escort, the T 36, under Lieutenant Commander Robert Hering, and followed her at full speed. The T 36 was loaded down with military stores and machine parts. She also carried 250 refugees.

The two warships rounded the northern tip of Pomerania some time after 2000 hours, and set a westerly course. Forty-five minutes later a look-out on the T 36 reported seeing distress signals from a ship to the west and soon afterwards the radio officer sent up to the Captain the *Gustloff*'s SOS signal.

Captain Heningst of the *Hipper* at once ordered the T 36 to make top speed towards the reported position, promising that he would follow with his slower cruiser. The skipper of T 36 ordered action stations, and prepared his lifeboats for launching. It was almost an hour later before the warship sighted the *Wilhelm Gustloff*, listing and obviously settling. Commander Hering tried in vain to make contact with the Bridge of the liner before searching for the best place to go alongside.

But then it became clear that such a manoeuvre would crush survivors in the water between the two ships, so he decided to position himself a hundred metres behind the liner. He had just executed this move and stopped his engines when he heard the dreadful wail of the *Gustloff*'s sirens as she made her last plunge.

Hering had scrambling nets put out. Seamen wearing their oilskins clung to them trying to rope floating survivors and help them aboard. The ship's boats were also lowered to help with the rescue work.

More rescue ships were heading for the scene. Had the *Gustloff* managed to stay afloat even a little longer, many more of the passengers would have been rescued. But once she had gone down the chances of survival were not great even for those who had managed to get into the boats and rafts. For those floating in the sea, which was spattered with small ice floes, they were virtually nil.

Most died almost immediately of exposure. Others were killed fighting for places in the boats and rafts. There were those willing to club each other to death to get out of the water; armed men in boats opened fire when swimmers threatened their already overloaded craft.

The raft into which Commander Zahn finally collapsed had only one sailor aboard, and he was struggling to save another life. In the mesh of webbing which formed the bottom of the raft was the head of a moaning girl. She had clutched at the raft as she came to the surface from immediately beneath it and caught her head in the straps. Her mouth was just above the water, the rest of her body floated underneath.

The sailor could not pull the straps apart, and neither he nor Zahn had a knife to cut them. Despite her screams they did the only thing possible. They pushed her head down, then reached beneath the raft to try to grab her body. They failed. She disappeared.

Shivering and exhausted, Zahn now saw an empty lifeboat floating nearby. He made a jump for it and hauled himself in, only to find that it was a boat without a bottom. He had to cling to this highly unsatisfactory craft for some time until he saw another boat near at hand.

Once again he launched himself into the water and swam to the boat, already filled with survivors. "Help!" he shouted, "Get me aboard!"

As the boat approached, a familiar face appeared over the gunwale. It was an engine room rating named Herbert Schulz, who recognised Zahn, and helped him into the boat.

This was the cutter in which Captain Petersen had so promptly reserved his place; the same boat into which Professor Bock had pulled Baroness von Maydell and her son. The young von Maydell had manfully taken his turn on the oars, but now he was exhausted.

Argument had raged about taking on more survivors, and many were opposed to running further risks by hauling in strangers who might upset the boat. So it was fortunate for Zahn that the rating had identified him. Not long after the wave had swilled them from the deck of the *Gustloff*, Professor Bock had had to intervene to save a woman's life.

"If we take any more we shall all die," Captain Petersen protested; and others attempted to strike at the woman's hands as she clutched the side. But Bock stood firm. "No," he cried. "We cannot leave her to drown." And he pulled her inboard.

"You had no right to do that," Petersen yelled.

"There were few people in the boat to start with," Ebbi von Maydell recalled. "But once we were among the swimmers away from the ship more and more people scrambled in until there must have been about fifty with us. Every time a fresh person clambered in there was more water in the boat. Already the snow in it had melted and we sat up to our knees in icy water. It seemed as if the boat might just fill up and turn over.

"Many figures floated silently past us in the water in their lifejackets. They were probably already dead. I know that later we had several corpses on board, women and children pulled out of the sea who were so exhausted that they just slumped forward and drowned in the water at the bottom of the boat.

"I remember that Professor Bock, who had taken over one of the oars and was sitting next to me, felt something under his feet. He told me later that it took some time for him to realise that it was the body of a drowned child. We were all so emotionally exhausted that such horrors did not register for a while.

"By this time the scene was lit at moments by a pale moon that kept appearing between scudding clouds which until then had blacked it out. It was in this eerie light that, after rowing for about an hour, we came to the T 36. It was already surrounded by boats and rafts."

Once aboard the torpedo boat they realised how cold they were. Professor Bock remembered that his legs were completely numb, although the rowing had kept the rest of his body comparatively warm.

Zahn made his way to the Bridge and spoke with Lieutenant Commander Hering. He found this officer deeply preoccupied, for he had just received a sonar report of submarines in the immediate vicinity.

Within minutes he would need to make decisions on which the safety of his ship and the lives of dozens of *Gustloff*'s survivors would depend.

T 36 had already stood by over an hour picking up survivors and she was now in a highly dangerous position if the Russians renewed their attack. The *Hipper*, which had followed Captain Hering's warship to the spot, made only a brief stop. Her Captain decided that his heavily-loaded cruiser, crammed with refugees already, should not be exposed to submarine attack. In any case the high, looming sides of the cruiser made it almost impossible for her to join in the rescue work. The Captain of the *Hipper* continued his journey westwards at speed. He ordered the T 36 to do all she could for the survivors and to stay as long as possible.

Bosun Schottes had taken command of one of the cutters floating away from the *Gustloff* and, as searchlights swung across the sea, he saw the *Hipper*'s approach. A number of swimmers and people on rafts were quite close to the cruiser. For this reason Schottes decided that if he were to bring his boat to the port side of the cruiser those in the sea might be in danger of getting crushed between him and the steel sides of the larger vessel. He therefore steered towards the starboard side of the cruiser, then ordered "easy oars" and waited for the *Hipper* to drop anchor.

After a few minutes he saw the sea foaming just ahead and knew that the big ship was not going to wait after all. He remembered hearing cries of horror as those in the sea were drawn in towards the screws which tore to pieces a number of *Gustloff* survivors just when they believed that they were about to be rescued. It was certainly not the fault of Captain Heningst. He had no choice but to put the safety of his own ship first once submarines had been detected nearby.

But to the hundreds of people still in the water it seemed the final betrayal.

"Because of the great submarine danger the ship had to sail on without picking up a single survivor," reported the Captain the following day when he reached Swinemunde. "Had the *Admiral Hipper* stayed on the spot she might easily have become yet another victim of U-boat attack."

21

CAPTAIN MARINESKO, THOUGH at this point having troubles of his own with the jammed torpedo tube, was presented with a fine opportunity to attack a capital ship of the German Navy. With the T 36 busy picking up survivors, the *Hipper*, almost at a standstill, presented an easy target for the submarine commander. But there is little doubt that the Soviet U-boat commander over-estimated the strength of her escort.

At this point there is an intriguing discrepancy in the accounts of survivors from the *Gustloff* and those given by Soviet sources. Heinz Schoen, in the course of his investigations into what happened to people from the *Gustloff* after the sinking, found a number of survivors who told him that while they were in the sea shortly after the sinking they saw the conning tower of a submarine and could actually hear sailors on it talking in Russian. But the S 13's log book records that by then Marinesko had taken his boat under water. Was there another submarine on the scene?

Certainly the Germans believed that the *Hipper* was in grave danger and she accordingly left the scene at high speed. So now the T 36 and the *Löwe* represented the only hope for the survivors who sped the *Hipper* on her way with despairing curses.

The sea was still dotted with bobbing heads of men and women held more or less above the waves by their lifejackets. As the cutter with Captain Petersen on board made its way towards the T 36, Gunther von Maydell, who was crying from cold and fright, noticed what he described as "whole islands of rafts. They were so close together that they looked like islands, many of them occupied by people."

When the cutter approached too closely to one of these

islands, someone on board, and he cannot remember who it was, said: "Keep away from them. They will all try and get into our boat and overturn us." Everybody was now a potential enemy in the battle for survival.

On board the T 36 the situation was still critical for Hering, anxiously receiving more reports of submarine activity while his crew were hauling numbed survivors aboard and reviving them with hot coffee. They were also helping some of the pregnant women who had reached the comparative safety of the torpedo boat. During the night after the rescue three babies were born on the ship with sailors acting as midwives under the professional guidance of Dr. Richter.

Commander Zahn, on the Bridge with Hering, was offering his expertise in the matter of U-boat warfare. The torpedo boat was drifting and would have been a soft target for any lurking submarine. Sonar picked up the position of the S 13. It was 1,400 metres away and coming towards them. Hering continued his rescue operation.

"The moment it comes within 800 metres you must get under way," Zahn warned him.

For the moment Hering contented himself with swinging his ship slowly, in order to keep his bows in line with the approaching submarine so that he presented the smallest possible target.

When sonar placed the submarine at under 1,000 metres, Hering decided he must take Zahn's advice. But before giving the order to move off he made one last attempt to warn those still in the sea, many of whom were bound to be the innocent victims of any rapid action on his part.

Taking a loud hailer he went to the wing of the Bridge and shouted down, "There is a submarine. We must leave but we'll be back. Hold on!"

Few in the water could have heard him, but at least he had tried to warn them and give some comfort. As he gave the engine room orders to move ahead and the diesels roared, two torpedoes were reported, one passing to starboard and the other to port. As the T 36 got under way the sonar detected a submarine under her stern.

Hering had moved so quickly that a number of his own crew on the nets and in the rescue boats were swept away and drowned, but he had succeeded in rescuing 550 people.

With these, and the 250 refugees already on board – including Hering's mother – the small warship was completely packed and it is doubtful whether there would have been room for more.

"Lieutenant Commander Hering and the T 36 acted magnificently and deserve special recognition," reported Commander Zahn later.

As the ship moved away, and again on Zahn's advice, T 36 fired practice depth charges. Indeed it is likely that she had very few real depth charges on board, and in any case she was manned by a scratch crew, few of whom had been trained for the complications of anti-submarine warfare. But even the practice depth charges, exploding in such conditions, were powerful enough to kill people swimming nearby.

The detonations terrified survivors on the warship, including Ebbi von Maydell. "I had sunk into a doze on the T 36, just thankful to be alive and warm, from which I was awoken by a loud explosion. This was followed by others, and with each one the ship seemed to jump in the water," she reported. A ship's officer soon reassured her and said that the warship was attacking the submarine with depth charges. The Baroness concluded her account: "Some of the ship-wrecked who were about to be taken on board were left to drift."

That is an understatement. The sudden movement of the torpedo boat mangled some of the survivors, and her bow wave was powerful enough to throw others out of their rafts.

Rudi Lange was drifting in the sea not far away. "I was terrified by the noise," he said later. "Every explosion seemed to shatter my eardrums."

He had been among the last to leave the liner, having

stayed behind as long as possible to continue transmitting the SOS.

"In the final stages my hands were so cold that the portable transmitter kept slipping away from me on the Bridge. I thought that my last hour had come. I crawled across the deck and finally got into a liferaft stuck on the deck and just hoped for the best. A big wave swept it and me off the deck and then I remember swimming through a sea of corpses."

The T 36 was already moving and the *Löwe* was preparing to leave when its searchlight picked out Lange. He shouted for help, and soon sailors from the *Löwe* were hauling him aboard. "I fainted, and knew nothing until I was lying on a bunk. Sailors were cutting my uniform away from me because it was stiff with ice."

Lange was almost the last survivor picked up by the *Löwe* before she, too, left the scene of the disaster. This small escort vessel had already rescued 252 people, including Gertrud Agnesons, the Navy girl who had fought her way up from below decks, and Maria Kupfer, the sole survivor of the hundreds herded into the Lower Promenade Deck. The *Löwe* also had on board Louis Reese, the first officer, and captain of the watch Heinz Kohler. She sailed for Kolberg.

After ending her rescue operation the T 36 circled in the area for another twenty minutes, firing her practice depth charges. Then, as Commander Zahn, worn out by the experiences of the night, went below to rest, she made off at seventeen knots. At 0430 on January 31st, she caught up with the *Admiral Hipper* and by 1400 hours she arrived at Sassnitz on the island of Rugen, where a Danish hospital ship, the *Crown Prince Olav*, was waiting to take on board the *Gustloff* survivors.

Those rescued by the T 36 were the lucky ones. There were dozens whose ordeal lasted much longer.

When Walter Knust finally managed to push his small boat away from the side of the *Gustloff* he found it difficult to get his oar down into the water, so crowded was the sea with swimming survivors. For the first few minutes they did nothing but haul in as many people as possible. "It was a small boat with a normal capacity for about eighteen people. Finally there were at least thirty-six of us packed in, and we were so low in the water that only fifteen centimetres separated the top of the gunwales from the sea," said Herr Knust. The only advantage of being in that boat was that it had a small cabin, built to house a radio operator, and this afforded some protection.

But another unpleasant surprise awaited the engineer officer as he and Roger tried to organise things in the boat. There were no rowlocks for the oars, so he had to improvise some with rope. Thus equipped, they pulled away from the ship.

Even so Knust was not happy with his craft and feared that it was so overloaded that it might sink. When he saw another boat nearby, he said to his wife, who was close to him: "Let's change boats." But before they could do so a man he knew in the other boat shouted: "Herr Knust, we are sinking."

"What's the matter?" asked Knust, and they told him that the drainage bungs in the bottom of the lifeboat were missing. The boat was taking in water and Knust told them to get handkerchiefs and bits of material to fill the bung holes. After the war he wondered whether this lifeboat had not been deliberately sabotaged, possibly by Polish dock-workers.

"Our boat did have a compass," said Knust, "so I steered south knowing that land lay in that direction. One of the seamen with us suggested that we should try to start the diesel motor, but I told him it would be best to keep that in reserve because we never knew when we might really need it."

Paula Maria Knust remembers sitting huddled in the boat with a pullover wrapped round her while her husband got things organised with the help of the other men. She had no stockings and remembers the bitter cold, and how wet it was.

"When we had time to look around we found that some people in the boat were already dead. One sailor went mad and jumped into the sea. There was also a woman we had picked up who began screaming that she wanted to die, and we had to restrain her from jumping back into the sea. She had lost all her children. She was demented by grief."

A number of mothers who had seen their children die either killed themselves or literally died of grief. Among the latter was a woman in a small dinghy occupied by two sailors. According to their report, her eldest child had been killed by a blow from a heavy suitcase crashing down after the first explosion, then her eight-year-old boy was trampled to death in the stampede on a staircase. On deck the youngest child was snatched from her arms by a wave. Such horror proved too much for her and she died on the dinghy.

"I remember thinking at the time how strange were the different ways in which people reacted to the horror of that night," said Frau Knust. "Most people were in complete panic and just screamed hysterically. 'But what good does that do?' I asked myself.

"Some people were very brave. One of the few men in our boat jumped into another one which had only women and children in it. He took one of our oars in order to steer it."

After Knust had steered his boat south for a while he was relieved to spot the navigation lights of a ship not far away. "I called to one of the men to wave his torch in that direction, but nothing happened.

"He said, 'I have a gun with me, shall I shoot?'

" 'OK,' I said, 'but only one bullet. You just don't know when we may need the others.' Anyway he fired and somebody must have heard the shot, for about five minutes later we could see the lights moving towards us."

It was the TS 2, a torpedo recovery vessel commanded by a naval officer called Brickmann, who had made his way to the scene. The time was almost 0300 on the morning of January 31st and the Knusts and their fellow passengers had been rowing and drifting for nearly five hours.

"It was terrifying because the waves swept us up high and level with the deck one minute and then threw us back: you had to choose just the right moment to jump for the deck," explained Frau Knust. "My husband shouted and told people when to try, then helped them with a push.

"I was second last to leave, and finally Walter jumped. He took me straight to the Captain's cabin where they gave me coffee and cognac. We were all scared by a new series of explosions. But it was just the TS 2 firing depth charges in case the submarine was still there as we sailed off towards Swinemunde."

But before he boarded the warship Walter Knust performed one more duty. He reported to the officers that he had three dead aboard his small boat.

"Leave them there," replied the first officer. "They will have the sea as their grave."

Herr Knust talked to the Captain for a while over schnapps and a cigarette on the Bridge. He remembers with gratitude that the Captain gave him a whole pack of cigarettes. There was a seaman from the *Gustloff* already on board and he offered Knust, who had no socks, a pair of thigh-length submarine socks. "Later on my wife took the wool from them and knitted me two pullovers from it," said Knust.

Even aboard the TS 2 the troubles of the survivors were not yet over, for at dawn they were very nearly blown up by a mine which destroyed a small minesweeper sailing just 500 yards ahead of them. "God was with us, for nobody had ordered that ship to go ahead," said Herr Knust.

To remind her of events that night Frau Knust still has in her possession a battered piece of wartime official paper handed to her before she was put ashore in Swinemunde. It reads: "This is to confirm that the bearer was rescued in the night of 30/31 January, 1945, as a shipwrecked person." It was signed by the commanding officer of the ship, First Lieutenant Brickmann, and duly marked with the official stamp of the TS 2.

Even in disaster naval officers stick to the routine laid down.

Just after midnight when the *Löwe* and T 36 had already sailed westwards a convoy consisting of the 5,266 ton freighter *Gotenland* and her escort, the minesearcher M 387, appeared on the scene. They had come from Libau and were sailing to Swinemunde with 4,000 refugees. Neither had heard any of the SOS messages but arrived there by chance, and busied themselves picking up survivors. Between them they rescued 106.

An hour later the 6,227 freighter *Göttingen*, and her escort the M 375, came up after being alerted by radio. The escort rescued fifty-four people and among the fifty-seven taken from the sea by the *Göttingen* was Eva Luck, the sixteen-year-old who found herself trapped in the music room with the rogue piano.

Sigrid Bergfeld, one of the very few naval auxiliary girls to escape, was rescued after hours in an open raft by the small naval vessel TF 19. Of the seven picked up by this vessel in the small hours of January 31st, only two were finally capable of walking ashore. The TF 19 had come out from Gdynia, and her skipper entered in his log book: "31st Jan. Noon – arrival in Gdynia, disembarkation of the *Gustloff* survivors." After all the horrors of the night, after surviving the most terrible sea disaster on record, this unfortunate group of seven had arrived back twenty-four hours later at precisely the place they had been so anxious to leave aboard the "safe ship" *Wilhelm Gustloff*.

Suffering from frostbitten legs, Sigrid Bergfeld and the others were taken to the military hospital at Gdynia – Oxhöft.

Guy Sajer, who wrote a moving account of his soldiering and suffering on the Eastern Front in *The Forgotten Soldier*, arrived in Gdynia about that time searching for the remnants of the Gross Deutschland Division to which he belonged. He wrote:

A rumour was circulating through the throng of refugees: a large ship had been sunk a few days earlier, almost certainly after a torpedo attack. It had been crammed with refugees, relieved to be escaping to a region of greater security. It was easy to imagine the horror of the scene, in the black and icy night.

The news of this disaster had been officially withheld, but had nonetheless penetrated to the anxious mob, for whom the sea route was the last hope of escape. The ship in question was thought to be the *Wilhelm Gustloff*.

So the news came by way of rumours and whisperings to anxious friends and relatives of those who had sailed on the *Gustloff*. It was announced more formally by Admiral Doenitz at the Führer's Conference on Naval Affairs in Berlin at 1600 hours on January 31st in these terms:

"In connection with the sinking of the passenger steamer *Wilhelm Gustloff* by submarine torpedoes on the outer route, north of the Stolpe Bank, the C-in-C Navy declares that with the extensive transports in the Baltic Sea it was realised from the start that there would be losses. Painful as any loss may be, it is very fortunate that more have not occurred. However, he must point out that Russian submarines are able to operate undisturbed in the Baltic Sea only because there are no German aircraft there to combat them. Because of the shortage of escort forces the Navy must restrict itself to direct protection of convoys. The only practical defence against submarines is the radar-equipped aircraft, the same weapon which enabled the enemy to paralyse our own submarine warfare . . .

"The Führer underlines the arguments of the C-in-C, Navy, and orders the Air Force to investigate how the matter can be remedied."

And that was that. There was an irony in the statement. Doenitz was the officer who earlier in the war had promulgated the notorious "Laconia order"* in 1942. This required not

* Doenitz issued this order after U-boats which had rescued Britons and Italian prisoners of war from the torpedoed *Laconia*, were attacked from the air despite the fact that they were showing the red cross and were towing life-

only that submarines should strike without warning, but also that they should do nothing to help the crews of sunken ships. "All attempts to rescue the crews of sunken ships should cease, including picking up men from the sea, righting capsized lifeboats, and supplying food and water."

Now it was the enemies of Nazi Germany who had the upper hand and they were fighting according to the same rules. There was certainly no thought in the mind of Commander Marinesko that he should make any attempt to help the crew and passengers of the liner he had torpedoed. As far as he was concerned, they were Fascists who deserved to die.

boats full of survivors. Doenitz successfully argued at his Nuremberg trial that the safety of his U-boats and their crews came first. However, at the time, his order was taken as yet another example of German frightfulness.

22

THE LAST POIGNANT rescue was made in the dawn of January
31st, 1945, after all but one of the rescuers had abandoned the
search. A worn-out naval despatch boat, the VP 1703,
commanded by a lieutenant of the reserve, was making her
way cautiously among the ice floes where the liner had sunk.
Her crew no longer believed that there were any survivors left
to rescue when the boat came across a lifeboat with people
huddled together unmoving. Petty Officer Werner Fisch
jumped in to inspect it, and found everybody in it, men and
women, frozen to death. But, half hidden under one of the
bodies, was a baby, blue with cold, but still alive. He brought
the boy out and slowly revived him in the warmth of the VP
1703's cabin. Nobody knew who the child belonged to and the
petty officer adopted him.

As T 36 came alongside the quay at Sassnitz, on a fine
though bitterly cold morning, those of the survivors still
capable of walking made their way down the gangway. Many
had to be carried off on stretchers. The authorities had made
arrangements for their transfer to the *Crown Prince Olav*,
already in the harbour. Lieutenant Commander Hering
watched sadly from the Bridge, and as the last of his
passengers went ashore he saluted.

Most of those who had been snatched from the sea were still
too dazed to remember what was happening to them. They
gathered helplessly on the pier, vaguely wondering what
would occur next. Most of them were taken aboard the
hospital ship to Swinemunde, where those fit to travel were
put ashore. Frau Knust told us what happened to her:

"My husband was a Hamburg man, and despite the bombing we decided to try to get back there. At the railway station

we got aboard a train. All the windows had been blown out in air raids. In our compartment were myself, another woman, and eight shipwrecked men including the first engineer and some stewards who had all come ashore at the same time. We were still wearing our lifejackets and I had only one tennis shoe on my feet.

"Then two SA stormtroopers came into the compartment and demanded to see our identity cards. We used to call the stormtroopers 'golden pheasants' because they looked so plump and brown in their uniforms. Of course, we had no identity cards. We had escaped from the *Gustloff* with no possessions at all, and after all we had been through, we just could not believe that these men were bullying us for papers.

"I thought this is really crazy. Now they're going to put us in a concentration camp because we lost our papers in a torpedoed ship. But they didn't; they simply said this train was for women and children only and they turned us off."

The party went back down to the docks and found a friendly ship's captain who took them on board, saying that he expected to sail further west soon. Then he told them he had heard there was a military hospital train passing through on the way to Hamburg. The senior medical officer allowed them on the train and after a three-day journey Frau Knust and her husband finally arrived in Hamburg. It was mid-February.

Swinemunde was crammed with refugees from Prussia and Pomerania even before the *Gustloff* survivors arrived there. The day after the sinking of the liner, Admiral Doenitz informed Hitler that the town was filled with 20,000 refugees and more were arriving every day. Because they endangered troop transports from Courland, he considered it necessary to evacuate them once again. Accordingly, the Führer instructed Martin Bormann to disperse the refugees among the surrounding villages and to provide facilities to speed up the evacuation.

It was into this crowded place that Ebbi von Maydell and

her younger son Gunther were finally put ashore after all the rigours of the shipwreck. And here, while they were wandering through the town looking for somewhere to stay until they could move on westwards, one of those amazing wartime coincidences occurred. They bumped into Bernard, the Baroness's sixteen-year-old son, who had refused to go on board the *Gustloff* with his mother and brother. He had made his way overland to Swinemunde where he heard the first rumours about the sinking of the *Gustloff*. He had assumed that his mother and brother were dead and was amazed and overjoyed to find them again.

The *Löwe* made a shorter journey westwards than the T 36, putting her 252 survivors ashore at Kolberg in Pomerania, a dangerous haven, for it was soon threatened by the Russian advance. Even during that short voyage a number of people had died of exposure and shock. When the others went ashore a crowd of people, many of them refugees, gathered by the port to watch them pushing their way slowly through the snow-covered streets into the town. Many were plodding along in their stockinged feet, for they had lost everything when the *Gustloff* sank, and there was nobody to organise even a supply of boots and shoes.

Because naval personnel had been lost at sea, Commander Zahn, who had been the senior naval officer on board the *Gustloff*, was called to account before an official naval enquiry. The Board never pronounced decisively on the degree of his responsibility. The war was drawing to a close and the naval command had graver problems. But his naval career was finished. He ended his life as a salesman, embittered because he was convinced that he had done his best yet had been made a scapegoat in the disaster. Captain Petersen never went to sea again and died not long afterwards.

How many people actually died in the sinking of the *Wilhelm Gustloff*? Nobody knows, for in the end nobody can say how many people actually sailed in her, despite the attempts to keep control of the refugees and to count the people who struggled to get on board. First Officer Reese put the official total at 6,050 just before she sailed, but after that came the last-minute boardings from small craft which Rudi Lange estimated at some 2,000, making a total of over 8,000. It is known that 964 people were picked out of the sea, some of whom died later. It is likely, therefore, that at least 7,000 people perished.

Sea lawyers have argued since about the rights and wrongs of the sinking of the *Gustloff*. Many Germans have told the authors how wicked it was of the Russians to sink a refugee ship with so many women and children on board; and there is no doubt that thousands of innocent people perished in the disaster. Afterwards the Institut für Seerecht at Kiel, a body that studies naval and maritime law, was asked for an opinion. In a letter to Heinz Schoen, the historian of the *Gustloff*, they made clear their view. The Institut considered that the *Gustloff* was a legitimate target, a military vessel in the sense that it was transporting hundreds of naval submarine specialists. The *Gustloff*, though it also had wounded aboard, was not a recognised hospital ship; and the liner was armed with anti-aircraft guns.

Such thoughts seemed highly academic to those who had survived the horror of torpedoeing at sea, and equally so to those Germans on the Baltic coast who for weeks after January 30th found hundreds of frozen bodies washed up on the beaches.

Stab Führerin Wilhelmina Reitsch, who had so carefully chosen the Women's Naval Auxiliaries under her command for places aboard the "safe" evacuation ship, was still in Gdynia. To her fell the task of ordering her officers to identify the bodies.

23

WHILE THE INITIAL rescue attempts were being made, Marinesko was busy taking his boat out of danger. There are considerable discrepancies between the German and Russian accounts of what happened in the confused hours after the sinking. According to the Germans the S 13 or another Russian submarine made at least one attack on the T 36, and posed such a threat to the *Hipper* that she was forced to flee. But the Russian archives show no record of a follow-up attack. All their published accounts speak only of the S 13's escape under heavy depth charge attack.

After the war Redkobodorov recalled in *Evening Leningrad* that:

It was the most terrible time the crew of the S 13 ever faced. They hunted for us for just over four hours and dropped 234 depth charges in order to avenge the death of the liner. We alway liked to operate at least at a depth of 40 metres in those sort of circumstances, but at one time we were pushed to close to the shore that the depth was only about fifteen metres. It was only Marinesko's experience, intelligence and intuition which got us out of trouble.

Other accounts tell of Schnaptsev hearing the first depth charges a long way off and passing the word to Krylov who had the job of counting them with short pencil strokes on a piece of paper in groups of ten, of asdic signals "striking the S 13's hull like hail", and of one explosion that rattled their teeth, shattering several light bulbs and breaking dials in the control room.

And yet we know that the *Löwe*'s detection gear was frozen

and the T 36 only had practice depth charges and was too overloaded to fight.

It seems that both sides exaggerated their danger and that Marinesko missed an opportunity to sink the *Admiral Hipper*, while the "torpedoes" that caused the T 36 to abandon her rescue operations did not exist but were a trick of moonlight and waves combining to give the appearance of torpedo tracks.

It is, however, likely that the T 36 did pick up the S 13 on its sonar, for Marinesko decided to work back through the scene of the sinking in order to confuse the enemy ships he was sure would be hunting for him.

At all events, by 0400 hours on Wednesday, January 31st, Marinesko decided he had shaken off the Germans. No more depth charges were heard and Schnaptsev could pick up no propeller noise. Running quietly, the S 13 worked her way offshore and reached the comfort of open water.

Marinesko came up to periscope depth and searched the horizon. He could see no pursuers, but he still decided that it was too dangerous to surface, recharge his batteries and signal his success. His decision would mean a day of added discomfort for the crew, and Kronstadt would still not know where he was or what he had been doing. But the risks of surfacing were too great.

He waited till nightfall, then signalled to Kronstadt: "30 Jan. 55 degrees 02' 02'. 18 degrees 11' 05'. 2308. Three torpedoes fired from surface. All hit. Definitely sunk liner estimated 20,000 tons. Counter-attacked for four hours by several vessels. No damage. Remaining on station."

Captain Kurnikov read this signal with some scepticism. He asked if any intelligence reports had come in confirming the sinking of a large vessel off Hela, and was told there had been none. Kurnikov therefore decided that Marinesko was exaggerating. There had been no evidence from any source of the presence at sea of a liner of 20,000 tons. They would need to know a lot more about the incident before passing on a report to Moscow. It was up to the people there to decide what was announced and what was not. Even propaganda claims had to have a grain of truth in them. So he ignored Marinesko's signal, and sent one of his own to the S 13. It told the crew that on Saturday, January 27th, Leningrad had been awarded the Order of Lenin at a ceremony held in the Kirov Theatre.

Marinesko resumed his patrol. Still not knowing the name of the ship he had sunk or the magnitude of the disaster he had brought about, he had taken the S 13 into the quieter waters of the deep Baltic where he patched up his hard-run boat. The compass had failed and he was unable to navigate correctly until it was repaired by Petty Officer Electrician Yuri Ivanov. Marinesko also gave the order to reload the empty torpedo tubes.

This was a dirty and arduous job. Using blocks and tackle and hauling like a tug-of-war team, the torpedo men laboured to ease one and a half tons of steel and explosive into each of the tubes. It took time, and, according to his crew, Marinesko fretted throughout the operation, urging them on, anxious to get back to the fight. He has left no account of his feelings at this time but it is not difficult to imagine his determination to wipe out the shame of what had happened at Turku and his need to chalk up more successes despite the fact that he knew that he had sunk the biggest ship ever destroyed by a Russian submarine.

With the S 13 warworthy again, he patrolled along the edge of the convoy lanes during the day and moved in at night to take up position off the Stolpe Bank. His plan was to ambush any ships unwise enough, like the *Gustloff*, to move out without a proper escort, and to pick up convoys hugging the coastline on the other side of the bank. It was a procedure which had its hazardous moments. On February 6th, as he was running on the surface past the Hela lighthouse while banks of fog rolled across a calm sea, a German U-boat suddenly emerged from the fog and passed by the S 13 only five metres away. Yefremenkov, who was on the conning tower, stared in amazement at the German watch officers as they sailed past with the two conning towers almost touching. He heard the sound of a machine gun being cocked. But by the time the gunners had recovered from their surprise, the two submarines had disappeared from each other's sight, slipping into the concealing fog.

24

FEBRUARY WAS A busy month. Half a million people, soldiers and fleeing civilians, were transported by sea to the West. It was a bitterly cold time of bright, almost arctic weather. The ports were blocked by ice, and breakers were needed to crunch a passage for the ships.

Even before the *Wilhelm Gustloff* sailed the Russians had broken through to the coast and were threatening the ports of Danzig and Gdynia. With the departure of the last of the submarine training units the headquarters of the convoy escort groups moved from the naval base across the bay to Hela. Commander Bartels and his boss, Admiral Burchardi, set up their headquarters in a dug-out near the port. Their task now was to use small boats and fishing vessels to bring refugees from the southern shore of the Bay of Danzig and then try to ship them out on larger ships through Hela.

Originally inhabited by a few hundred fishermen, the Hela peninsula was now filled with thousands of refugees and was under constant Soviet artillery fire and bombardment from the air.

The other remaining centre for the evacuation was Pillau at the eastern end of the Bay of Danzig, only twelve miles from Königsberg. For some weeks the city had been almost surrounded, though wounded soldiers and refugees were still able to escape either by road or by crossing the frozen Frisches Haff. Pillau was also the refuge for another great influx of broken troops and battered civilians who arrived there by sea from Courland, where the battle still raged.

In the port, hard-pressed naval evacuation groups, and doctors and nurses almost overwhelmed by the succeeding waves of wounded and refugees, struggled to bring some sort of order out of the chaos. Towards the end, Pillau was under daily attack from the Soviet Air Force. In spite of all these difficulties, the evacuation ships still arrived from the West, and endured everything the Russians could fire at them or drop on them.

Three-quarters of each shipload were civilians, the rest were wounded soldiers. The soldiers had been sorted into two categories: those who had no chance of surviving, and those who might recover. The latter were embarked; the former were left to die.

For every thousand taken on board the rescue ships another three thousand poured into the port area. They had terrible tales to tell of the treks and of families lost along the way. Those with any strength left set out again across the frozen strip of water separating them from Danzig – it was farther away from the Russians and the refugees thought that they stood more chance of being rescued from there than from Pillau. The others waited forlornly for the ships to come. They queued before the wrecked buildings where the authorities boiled cauldrons of porridge to feed the helpless. There was meat to be had – the goats and cattle that had made the trek with their owners. A soldier reported that the most pathetic sight was that of the children who had lost their parents. "Even their tears froze."

Indeed, small children became pawns in an appalling survival game being played out in Pillau. In the early stages of the evacuation the order had been made that men and women with children should be given priority for places on the refugee ships. But, as we have already described, people were so desperate that mothers already on board were persuaded to throw down their babies to relations on the quayside, who used them again as boarding vouchers. Sometimes the infants fell into the water between ship and quay; more often they were trampled in the rush to catch them, as strangers grabbed for them, fragile passports to safety.

An army chaplain named Dorfmüller who had arrived in

the port in mid-January reported that he had never seen such terrible things. Children were stolen from beside their sleeping mothers. There were accounts of deserters snatching children in order to claim that they should be allowed on to the ships to save their "families". Some dressed as women to escape SS guards.

When Dorfmüller arrived in Pillau, his first impression was that things seemed entirely normal. But as he walked the streets, helping people as best he could, he was shocked by the change that came over the town and the people when the first waves of refugees began arriving in the middle of January. By the end of the month every building was packed with frightened people, and the tales they brought spread fear like an infection. On January 26th an ammunition dump in the fort blew up, and the explosion caused such destruction that scarcely a building in Pillau was left undamaged. Hundreds of people were killed, for on the night of the blast 28,000 refugees had trekked into the town.

Ten days after the explosion the first Russian bombers appeared. They met no opposition from the German fighters which only a few months before would have knocked them out of the sky. The formidable Messerschmitt 109s and Focke Wulf 190s were grounded for lack of fuel. The Russians rained down bombs, turning the already damaged town into ruins and rubble, pervaded by the smell of burning and death. As the refugee treks from Königsberg and the Frische Nehrung came in, they too were bombed and machine gunned.

Yet nothing could hold back the flood of refugees, such was their terror of the Russians. The German sailors responded to their plight with heroism coupled with organisational genius. They scraped together an armada of ships, some of them imposing liners, others tiny freighters fit only for the breaker's yard. They used anything that had guns as escort ships and plied backwards and forwards along the Pomeranian coast, under constant attack, but always coming back for more – more punishment, more losses and more refugees. They sailed mostly at night to avoid the Russian Air Force which was deadly by day but which still lacked the radar that would have enabled them to operate efficiently after dark. That, rather, was the submariners' hour. Yet despite the heavy traffic, the Russian submariners were relatively unsuccessful.

One ship that came under fire was the *Cap Arkona*, and her story is particularly tragic and strange. Twice Captain Konovalov in L 3, a minelaying submarine, tried to sink her. Twice he failed. Finally she was sunk off Lübeck Bay by rocket-firing Typhoon fighter-bombers of the RAF on May 3rd. The tragedy of this sinking is that she was carrying some 5,000 detainees from the concentration camps in Poland. So, with freedom in sight, and after enduring unspeakable horrors, most of these concentration camp victims died trapped on the liner which might have carried them to a new life.

British commandos who captured Lübeck shortly afterwards, when the bay was filled with the floating bodies of the *Cap Arkona* victims, were so enraged by the conditions of the few concentrations camp survivors that one of them took Field Marshal Ernst Milch, who had surrendered in full regalia, to look at them. The commando wrenched the Field Marshal's baton away from him and beat him about the head with it until the baton broke.

From the end of February until the beginning of March another Soviet submarine, the ocean-going K 52, under the command of Captain Third Class Travkin, was also operational in the area of the Stolpe Bank. He reported making six attacks during this period, and claimed to have sunk five ships and one torpedo boat. But none of these sinkings is confirmed by German records.

It fell to Marinesko to sink the next big ship. He struck on February 9th, the thirtieth day of his patrol. Schnaptsev found the convoy first, picking up propeller noises just before midnight. He passed on the news to Marinesko who was on the conning tower with the submarine's doctor, Lieutenant

Georgi Stepanenko, and Leading Seaman Georgi Zelyentsov. They swept the horizon with night glasses until Zelyentsov spotted some curious lights just above the surface of the sea. Marinesko ordered the crew to action stations and prepared to stalk the convoy before attacking on the surface. But this time it was not so easy. One of the escort vessels suddenly turned and steamed at full speed towards the S 13. Marinesko crash-dived and took evasive action. It was an hour before he was able to resume his stalk.

According to Chief Engineer Kovalenko, writing in *Red Star* later that year, the target was selected when Marinesko got within 4,000 metres of the convoy.

> The commander was convinced we had come across a cruiser of the *Emden* type, but the ship identification book did not help him determine which one it was. He kept saying to the others on the conning tower that it was about 15,000 tons and so they would sink this one and then go home. But this time he decided to get in close submerged and sink it with his stern torpedoes so that when the two escort vessels came for him he would be already diving deep and running.

The two torpedoes in the stern tubes were fired at 0250 hours (Russian time) and on this occasion there was no hitch. Both ran true, and through his periscope Marinesko watched them explode against the side of the ship. She sank almost immediately and as she did so a third explosion boomed back across the water. Marinesko thought it was either a boiler or the ammunition magazine. He turned the S 13 and disappeared into the Baltic.

The ship he had sunk was not a cruiser but the *General Steuben*, a 17,500 ton luxury liner belonging to North German Lloyd. She was not a modern ship, her two high funnels revealed her age, and it may have been these which confused Marinesko. She had been built by Stettiner Vulkan in 1922 and launched as the *München*, but her name was changed to the *General Steuben* after a fire on board in the 1930s. As in the case of the *Wilhelm Gustloff*, there was a significance in the name chosen. Her owners planned to operate her on the North Atlantic run to New York and so a name with German and American connotations was needed. Few could have been more appropriate than the one decided upon, for Baron Friedrich von Steuben was a Prussian general who became Grand Marshal to the Prince of Hohenzollern, and then, in 1777, was persuaded by his friend Saint Germain, the French Minister of War, to offer his services as drill master to the American revolutionaries, then sorely in need of instruction in military tactics. His offer was accepted and he began his work with Washington's troops at Valley Forge. One of his duties was unpalatable: he sat as a member of the court martial that ordered the hanging of the British spy, Major John André, a man of such engaging personality that even his enemies wept when he was executed. General Steuben became an American citizen after the men he had taught won their independence, and he spent his last years in a town named after him, Steubenville, in New York State.

The liner – described like the *Gustloff* as a *"sicher"* (well-found) ship – was popular on the Atlantic run and her solid silhouette was well known in New York, where the grand ships tied up in impressive array at the piers below the skyscrapers. How exciting those arrivals and departures were, with streamers and last minute champagne parties and shouts of "All ashore who's going ashore", while the sailing gongs sounded. But war changes all things. The *Steuben* had spent the last four years tied up at a very different port, being used, like the *Gustloff*, as an accommodation ship for the submariners. Now, there was no question of persuading people to "go ashore". Everybody was determined to embark.

The *Steuben* made a successful three-day run from Pillau to Swinemunde, setting out only a couple of days after the *Gustloff* had been sunk. Nurse Hildegard Schneider, now a secretary in Göttingen, one of the lucky ones on board the liner on that trip, told the authors of her experiences. She arrived in Pillau with a hospital train loaded with hundreds of wounded. They were kept in a siding near the docks for nearly a week while they waited for the liner to arrive from Gdynia to pick them up. Fifteen nurses did their best for the soldiers in appalling conditions; there was little food, the doctors had run out of drugs, the wounded had nothing to ease their suffering, they had even run out of the paper bandages which, by this time, were all that Germany could produce to bind its soldiers' wounds.

"No preparations had been made," said Nurse Schneider. "We had to beg for food from warships in the harbour. The only efficient thing was the transfer of our wounded to the ship which was carried out in a few hours by the army. We sailed the same evening."

The ship sailed in convoy, but her escorts left her when it was judged that she had passed the danger zone. They had other work to do. A number of the wounded died on board, but apart from that the journey was as uneventful as such a harrowing voyage could be. The wounded were swiftly unloaded and the *Steuben* prepared to sail back to Pillau.

She ran into fog on the return and was held up for twenty-four hours, eventually arriving at Pillau on February 8th. She could hardly have docked at a more dramatic moment, for word was spreading among the milling thousands around the docks that the Russians had broken through the defences before Königsberg. There was little time left. The *Steuben* immediately began taking another cargo of wounded on board, with battered ambulances bringing them directly from the front line to the docks, while the increasingly fearful civilian refugees threatened to force their way on board. The most seriously wounded soldiers were laid on the upper decks with their stretchers, head to toe, covering the Promenade Deck. The less badly wounded went below with the tide of refugees which was flowing into every nook and cranny in the ship.

By noon on February 9th, she had taken on board at least two thousand wounded and one thousand refugees. These figures are estimates made at the time, for by now there was no possibility of proper manifests being compiled. It is known that the crew numbered 450, including thirty doctors and 320 nurses to care for the wounded. This left only a hundred men to run the ship.

By now the scene was familiar to the weary naval officers in charge of the evacuation. At 1530 tugs pulled and pushed the liner out of harbour and she sailed to meet her escort. Only two small ships could be found for the task: an old torpedo boat, the T 196, and an even more ancient torpedo recovery ship, the TF 10. The torpedo boat was carrying two hundred refugees who had arrived from Königsberg, and were taken on at the last minute. They almost swamped her.

The sea was calm, but the sky was heavy with snow as the convoy began its voyage. Suddenly, two Russian fighters swooped out of the clouds to machine gun the T 196. The torpedo boat returned their fire and they did no great damage. However, by this time the Russian planes had established liaison with the submarines lurking off the Stolpe Bank. As they disappeared into the cloud, their radios would have passed the message that another convoy was moving out – and that there was only one route it could take.

The convoy commander was well aware of the danger, and as they turned out of Danzig Bay on the first hazardous leg of the voyage, all three ships began sailing a zig-zag pattern at full speed – it was one of these manoeuvres that had caused Marinesko to crash dive. In her efforts to maintain speed to keep up with the *Steuben*, the coal-burning TF 10's ancient engines puffed out streams of bright sparks. These were the curious lights which Georgi Zelyentsov saw from the conning tower of the S 13 and led Marinesko to his second victim. His torpedoes hit the *Steuben* at 0053 hours (German time) on February 10th, striking the starboard side below the Bridge and below the aft funnel.

The T 196 turned to attack the submarine, but Marinesko was already moving out of harm's way when the first pattern of depth charges rumbled down. Lieutenant Hartig, Captain of the T 196, abandoned the chase and turned back to the *Steuben*. In the beam of his searchlight he could see her listing to starboard and beginning to sink, with her bows sliding quickly under the water while the wounded lay helpless, strapped to their stretchers, as the water engulfed them.

Hartig fired distress rockets but there was little else he could do except stand by to pick up survivors, and it was all over in seven minutes. There was no time to organise the passengers – many of whom were too badly wounded to help themselves – and the crew stood no chance of getting the life-boats away.

Only a handful of those in the forward part of the liner could reach the upper decks. Many of the soldiers realised this and, tired of struggling for life, shot themselves on their stretchers. Those on the upper decks able to do so ran aft as the ship's stern rose high out of the water. They hoped that the bows would come to rest on the sea bed and that part of the ship would remain above water. But she turned on her side just before she sank and they stood no chance. Many of those who jumped from the stern as she went down were torn to pieces by the still turning propellers. It is estimated that 3,000 died in those seven minutes. As the *General Steuben* went under, a great scream issued from the people trapped aboard. It was something the men on the escorting warships never forgot.

The best account of what it felt like to be on board the *Steuben* in those terrible moments comes from Franz Huber, one of the very few wounded to survive. He later became director of an insurance company, and told Fritz Brustat-Naval the naval historian, of his experiences.

He was suffering from head wounds sustained in a grenade attack near Pillau and was in great pain while he was being taken by ambulance to the dock-side to board the ship. There, he was treated and laid on one of the close-packed mattresses in the lounge with dozens of other head-wound patients.

Men around him were dying as the ship got under way, while he began trying to clean the grime and blood of battle from his face for the first time for a week. He was woken from fitful sleep by the exploding torpedoes.

"The whole ship shivered and vibrated. People were screaming and shouting. The ship rocked violently and those wounded men still capable of getting up were thrown against the sides. The rest just slid about while we somersaulted, fell on each other, and made our wounds even worse. But somehow I managed to put on my lifejacket."

He was one of the few who succeeded in making his way to the top deck where he saw hundreds of wounded, doctors and nurses, women and children, jumping into the sea.

"I sat there in the dark alone and heard screams from all over. I heard them praying the Lord's Prayer in such a voice as I will never hear again. Somewhere the ship was burning and people everywhere were jumping into the water."

As the *Steuben*'s stern rose out of the water, Huber, too, jumped and swam to a rubber dinghy with three others, including a German Red Cross nurse. One man was already in it; an odious sergeant major who made no attempt to help anyone, even the nurse. When they saw spotlights on the water nearby the NCO was convinced that it came from the Russian submarine and that the Russians intended to take him prisoner and send him off to Siberia.

Huber and his companions drifted for more than five hours in the bitterly cold night before the dinghy was spotted by the T 196 and they were taken on board the warship, more dead than alive.

Indeed most of those who had jumped into the sea died of cold and exposure. Only three hundred of those picked up by the escorting warships survived the voyage to Kolberg, where they were disembarked. The warships abandoned the scene at dawn. There was nothing more to be done.

25

So COMMANDER MARINESKO had destroyed two of Germany's largest liners within ten days and in doing so had killed more than ten thousand people. There is no evidence to show that he felt any compassion for them or regret at what he had done. As far as the Soviet Union was concerned those ten thousand, even though they included women and children and wounded, represented a division of Fascists. And after what they had done to Russia there could be no compassion. It was truly a case of "blood for blood". Marinesko had, of course, more personal reasons for delighting in his success. He had become the "tonnage king" of the Red Navy, he had vindicated his theories, and he had wiped out the events of Turku.

Three days later he received a signal giving him permission to return to the Smolny base. By now he had little of his 110 tons of fuel left, he was running short of torpedoes, and after a patrol that had already lasted thirty-five days the crew were tired and so was the S 13. He turned for home.

Two days later he neared Turku. Coming within sight of the masts of a sunken Dutch cargo steamer at the entrance to the port, he fired two blank rounds to mark his two successes. An ice-breaker crashed open a channel for the S 13 and he brought it into dock.

As soon as the S 13 was tied up his colleagues, experienced submariners all, climbed on board to welcome him. They had heard of his claims and believed him. The commanders of the other submarines at the base kissed him on both cheeks, pumped his hand, and slapped him on the shoulder.

Captain Oryel told him that, according to the Swedish newspaper *Stockholm Tidningen* he had sunk the *Wilhelm Gustloff*. It also appeared that he had sunk the *General Steuben* and not a cruiser. The S 13, said Oryel, would be given credit for both achievements.

It had become a tradition in the Baltic submarine flotilla that the success of a commander was celebrated with a dinner. Each member of the crew was allowed to bring as many guests as ships the submarine had sunk. The high-light of the banquet was when the cook brought in a dish on which lay a roast sucking pig, its legs in the air, bound up in blue ribbon. There would be toasts, speeches and singing.

There was a dinner for Marinesko, but no sucking pig. They said none was available. "Later," they told him, "when you become a Hero of the Soviet Union . . ."

26

THE DAY AFTER the sinking of the *General Steuben*, Admiral Doenitz made a concise report at the Führer's Naval Conference: "In connection with the loss of the hospital ship *Steuben*, the C-in-C Navy reports that in spite of regrettable losses, the use of large ships for evacuating the wounded from the Eastern Area cannot be dispensed with. Otherwise the possibility of transporting the wounded would be reduced by about 40,000 a month; the small ships available could carry about 17,000 in all. In fact, a total of about 76,000 wounded has been transferred West by water from the Eastern Area up to the present time, and losses represent only a small percentage in comparison."

It is significant that he should stress the importance of bringing out the wounded. He no doubt wished to impress Hitler, who still, at this late stage, believed that the war must continue and wanted these men, when healed, to carry it on. But Doenitz himself no longer had any illusions. He knew the war was over. His one aim now was to get as many people as possible away from the Russians, and bringing back the wounded was merely his pretext for this. Later, when he succeeded Hitler, he kept the war going in the West, refusing to capitulate to the demands for unconditional surrender because such a surrender would freeze all movement and end the rescue operation. He told the authors how grateful he was when Field Marshal Montgomery signed a separate surrender agreement which allowed the evacuation to continue for two more days until the final capitulation on May 9th. Doenitz's fame rests on his advocacy of submarine warfare and his moment of prominence as Hitler's heir. In reality, however, his main achievement lay elsewhere. He was nothing less than the architect of the greatest seaborne evacuation in history.

In the early spring he concentrated his naval and shipping resources and used his dwindling reserves of coal and oil for this task. By mid-April the Russians had advanced into Gdynia and Danzig and other Soviet armies were far into Pomerania. Earlier in the month they had broken into Königsberg. Thirty divisions finally overwhelmed the city and the area round it, and the city itself was in ruins when General Lasch, who was in charge of the defence and had been wounded in the course of it, surrendered on April 9th to spare the civilian population further suffering. He was promptly sentenced to death by Hitler, who had his family arrested by the SS as hostages. Meanwhile Gauleiter Koch had already undermined Lasch's position by keeping up a stream of messages to the Führer boasting of the fight he was maintaining and denouncing "traitors" who surrendered. A speech by Goebbels, relayed by radio to Königsberg, reflects the attitude of the Nazi hard-liners at this time. The Germans, he declared, could now say like the Romans: "*Hannibal ante portas.*" But they must remember there had been not one, but three Punic Wars, and in the end the Romans won. It may indeed have been this thought that prompted the navy to give the sailing of the *Gustloff* the code-word "Hannibal". Germany had suffered a setback; the enemy were at the gates. But Germany would triumph in the end.

This did not seem likely to the inhabitants of Königsberg when the Russians broke in. Count Hans von Lehndorff, a surgeon who was both anti-Nazi and deeply religious, has written a moving account of those days in his *East Prussian Diary*. He describes how life went on, with men tilling their fields while fighting was going on a few hundred yards away and women sweeping their steps as the Russians advanced along the nearby streets.

And then they arrived. The pictures Lehndorff paints of the scenes in his hospital are Dantesque:

. . . A wild howling mob was fighting over the finest tinned foods, and provisions that hundreds could have lived on for a whole year were being destroyed in a few hours . . . Stifled sounds of protest came from all the wards. Patients were being rolled out of bed and their bandages removed . . . One Russian, a mere lad, suddenly burst into tears because he hadn't yet found a watch. He held up three fingers; he would shoot three men if he didn't get a watch at once . . . A couple of nurses who got in their way were seized and outraged from behind and then released again, thoroughly dishevelled, before they realised what was happening . . . The town had been delivered up to the troops. I then realised that this was the first time during their campaign that women had fallen into their hands in any number . . .

Pockets of German soldiers and the never-ending army of refugees no longer had a safe port to make for once Pillau had fallen. There were only the sand dunes of Hela and a few "hedgehogs" along the coast left to them. The rearguards had their backs to the sea and the refugees huddled together on the beaches, waiting for small boats to ferry them out to the bigger ships which could not come inshore.

It was strikingly like Dunkirk. Russian fighters and bombers swooped on the dunes; Russian heavy artillery pounded the beaches. Now it was the Germans' turn to lie in the shell holes and wait to be taken off.

27

As the attack in Pomerania by the Second Byelo-Russian Front armies had developed and its spearhead reached westwards along the Baltic coast, naval operations had become even more hazardous for the Germans. In late February and early March the 2nd Battle Group concentrated on giving cover to the German bridgehead opposite Wollin. This task force comprised the pocket battleship *Admiral Scheer*, three destroyers and the torpedo boat T 36 which had earlier played such a notable part in rescuing survivors of the *Wilhelm Gustloff*.

Two destroyers and another torpedo boat gave support to the 3,000 troops in the tiny village of Kahlberg on the Frische Nehrung which, encircled since March 7th, had become the last evacuation centre. Their actions made it possible for naval landing craft flotillas to take off some 75,000 isolated refugees and embark them aboard larger warships and transports lying offshore. This last-minute operation was completed by the night of March 17th.

In the earlier fighting the German Second Army had been thrown back to a line stretching southwards from the sea at Rixhöft where, with the support of the big naval guns, it had managed to stabilise the front for a while, giving time for further evacuations. In early March the cruiser *Prinz Eugen* joined the old battleship *Schlesien* in bombarding Soviet positions ashore, but eventually the battleship had to withdraw when she ran out of ammunition.

To counteract these moves the Soviets put increasing air pressure on the German ships, using ground attack planes, along with torpedo and mining aircraft. These naval air units made no less than 2,023 sorties against embarkation opera-

tions in the Danzig-Gdynia area and off Hela. The only
defence against them was the AA barrage provided by
destroyers and other smaller craft of the German Fleet. A
number of transports were sunk, yet big liners, such as the
Deutschland, were still able to sail westwards carrying up to
11,000 people each.

Some losses were caused by Soviet submarines laying
mines off Hela. The L 21 under Captain Mogilevski who had
on board his Divisional Commander Captain Oryel – the
man who had saved Marinesko at Turku – was responsible
for one mining operation which sank a U-boat and two
torpedo boats.

Off the Stolpe Bank, now a notorious danger spot for the
Germans, the L 3, L 21 and K 53 were operating with varying
degrees of success, sniping at the convoys as the evacuation
built up in front of the Russian guns. The Germans themselves did something the Royal Navy and Royal Air Force
had been trying to do since the beginning of the war: sink the
Gneisenau. Just before Gdynia and Danzig fell on March 28th
and 30th, the badly damaged battleship was scuttled as a
blockship across the entrance to the naval base.

Then, early in April, "Operation Walpurgisnacht" was
mounted to rescue 8,000 men of the 7th Armoured Corps, cut
off at the Oxhöfter Kampe. This was carried out with a flotilla
of more than sixty landing craft and other small vessels which
took the soldiers across the bay to Hela. The same flotilla then
succeeded on the night of April 4th–5th in taking off no less
than 30,000 refugees from the Oxhöfter Kampe and transporting them to Hela. There, they were transferred to liners
and transports lying offshore under the protection of the guns
of the pocket battleship *Lützow*, supported by destroyers and
torpedo boats including the ubiquitous T 36.

Among the last to leave Hela aboard a destroyer was
Wilhelmina Reitsch, the Stab Führerin of the Women's Naval
Auxiliaries who had chosen the first of her girls to leave
aboard the *Gustloff* Colonel Count Karl zu Eulenberg, hus-

band of the Countess who had made her perilous journey earlier, was himself evacuated from here about Easter. "As we sailed westwards it was as though we were sailing through a graveyard of ships," he remembered. "You could see the wreckage of transports and warships everywhere along that coast."

Increasing Soviet air activity was now taking its toll, sinking altogether thirteen ships within a week at the beginning of April. To make things worse for the officers organising the evacuation, Soviet MTBs began operating from Neufahrwasser, near Gdynia, posing a new threat. Despite this, 264,887 people were evacuated from around the Bay of Danzig to Hela in the month of April.

German warships concentrated off Hela to provide the barrage of anti-aircraft fire needed to protect the refugee ships against attacks from the air.

Guy Sajer narrowly survived the fall of Gdynia and was evacuated to Hela at about this time. There was an air-raid warning as their boat pulled in and the cynical old soldier just did not believe a policeman who told them not to panic and assured them that the AA defences would hold off the raiders. In *The Forgotten Soldier* he writes:

> We hadn't quite reached shelter when the massive crackle of an anti-aircraft barrage burst all around us, fired by our coastal defences or by one of the warships we had glimpsed earlier. This was my first experience of such a barrage . . . We heard an explosion to the south, over the water; one of the planes must have been hit. The police had not been exaggerating – not one plane flew over Hela. We felt a wave of confidence and security; finally the Russians had been stopped.

However, the seaborne defences against air attack were effective only for a while, for first the *Lützow*, then several destroyers, had to withdraw because they ran short of fuel and ammunition, while others were damaged in the ceaseless raids.

Another big convoy left Hela on April 15th. It consisted of four liners and transports bearing 20,000 refugees and soldiers. In this convoy was the *Pretoria*, and crouched on the windswept bridge was Guy Sajer, hungry and thirsty, but glad that at last he was leaving the Eastern Front.

The faithful T 36 was one of the escorts for this convoy, but she broke away later to shepherd a damaged destroyer into Swinemunde.

28

THE FOLLOWING DAY another convoy was assembling at Hela for the run westwards, and now it was the turn of the 7th Tank Corps to be lifted. These soldiers were veterans of the siege of Leningrad and the long retreat back from the East. They were urgently needed, for it was planned that, reformed and equipped with new tanks, they would be thrown into the battle for Berlin. Among them was Captain Küspert with 200 survivors from the 35th Tank Regiment who had fought in the bitter defensive actions at the Weichsel bridgehead before being ferried to Hela. As they left they could see the smoke and flames rising from the shattered city of Danzig.

Russian planes were swarming over the pier area as a group of men from the Second Army, led by Lieutenant Brinkmann, boarded ships and lighters to take them out to the big ships of the convoy. It was 1000 hours on April 16th, and the lighter on which Brinkmann had found a place was heading for a 5,000 ton motorship, the *Goya*. As it approached the *Goya*, he saw a barge tied alongside with thirty or so elderly civilians, men and women, on it. Two bombs hit the barge. No one moved as it pulled away from the ship, but he noticed a trickle of blood running from the deck.

And just after dawn, the *Goya* herself had received a direct hit. A bomb tore open the deck and wounded her anti-aircraft gunners. The ship's master, Captain Plünneke, was asleep in his cabin at the time. He was wounded in the head by a bomb splinter. But both he and his ship were, in the circumstances of the time, still seaworthy, and they prepared to sail.

Hardened though he was to the horrors of war, Lieutenant Brinkmann was shocked by the scenes he witnessed as the *Goya* took on more and more refugees. She had embarked something like 7,000 people during the day, but more and more barges came and the pier was still packed with pleading refugees, as military equipment and baggage were hoisted on board. Finally Captain Plünneke gave the order that he could take only twenty more people. Among the last of them was a group of four, and Brinkmann heard a young man with his wife confronting the older man and woman who seemed to be his parents.

The young man, who had only one arm, screamed at them that they must stay behind because they were old and useless, whereas he and the girl had a lifetime before them. Under the dazed eyes of the old people, he and his wife climbed the scrambling nets up the side of the *Goya*, and never looked back at those they left behind.

The *Goya* raised anchor a little after 1900 hours and got under way to join the five other ships of the convoy and its meagre escort of two minesweepers for the long journey to Copenhagen. German ports in the Western Baltic were by then so overcrowded with shipping and refugees that the ships were being diverted to the occupied Danish capital.

The *Goya* was a modern ship, completed in 1942. Owned by the Hamburg America Line, she had been taken over by the German Navy. She was the biggest and fastest vessel in the convoy, and for this reason she took station to seaward as the convoy sailed. Air attacks during the day had sunk one small vessel, the *Boelcke*, near the entrance to the port and the convoy commander knew that the Soviet planes must have signalled details of the force's composition and sailing time both to their MTBs and submarines.

Engine trouble in some of the ships held up the convoy. When it got under way again the *Goya*, which could have made a much higher speed, had to slow down to nine knots to stay with the rest.

By the time they began to approach the critical Stolpe Bank area, night had fallen. There was no moon and few people were still above deck. One of the few was Lieutenant

166

Brinkmann who was on duty from 2200 hours until midnight. A few minutes before midnight he went up to the Bridge for the changing of the watch, at which time the *Goya* was some sixty miles off the coast of Pomerania, opposite the port of Stolpe.

Captain Third Class Vladimir Konstantinovitch Konovalov in his ancient minelaying L 3, which had failed to sink the *Cap Arkona*, was lying in wait. Tall, austere, and considered one of the most brilliant navigators in the submarine service, he had been second in command of the L 3 for three years before taking over as Captain in October 1944. The L 3 was at this time the most successful submarine in the entire Soviet fleet, having been credited with sinking four ships in 1941, six in 1942, and three, including the U-boat U 416, by mining in the first few months of 1943. Konovalov was destined for success. He knew Marinesko well and admired his courage and tenacity but he made no secret of his disapproval of the Odessan's swashbuckling image. He became a Rear Admiral before dying of a heart attack twenty years after the war and his two sons, Yevgenni and Mark, rose to command nuclear submarines – a far cry from the poorly constructed L 3 in which their father waited in ambush off the Stolpe Bank.

As Lieutenant Brinkmann made his way up the ladder to the *Goya*'s Bridge, Konovalov, scanning the sea through his periscope, made out the outline of the approaching ships. At 2356 he fired two torpedoes which hit the *Goya* amidships and astern.

All that the *Goya*'s officers and Brinkmann were aware of were two shattering explosions. Then the "abandon ship" signal was sounded and soldiers and refugees burst from the holds. But almost immediately, the ship broke in half and her masts crashed down on the struggling mass on deck. She took only four minutes to sink. Then she disappeared. To Konovalov, watching from the L 3, it was almost as if she had never existed.

But those on the *Goya* had time to agonise, and some even

to escape. A wave swept Brinkmann into the sea. Clutching at a liferaft he saw a jet of flame leap from the waves. The boilers had exploded. Then there was silence. As the rest of the convoy zig-zagged away into the night, all that the survivors could hear were screams and occasional pistol shots. Brinkmann drew his own pistol, then, overcoming his first impulse to shoot himself, he threw it away. After fighting off other soldiers trying to take his place on the raft he was eventually hauled out of the water by a rescue ship and taken to Copenhagen.

He was one of the very fortunate. Of the estimated 7,000 men and women on board, only 183 were rescued. Rarely can so many people have died so quickly. Captain Küspert was among those who perished, and only seven of his tank-men ever came to dry land. The 35th Tank Regiment ceased to exist.

According to Soviet accounts of the action, Captain Konovalov's submarine "was bombarded with depth charges but the lackey soldiers drowned beneath the weight of their weapons". It is difficult to believe that the bombardment was particularly effective, for the small escort craft can have mounted only a token counter-attack against the submarine.

The following day Konovalov was in action again in the same area. Soviet planes badly damaged a small gunboat, the *Robert Muller 6*, and the L 3 was called up to finish her off.

The sinking of the *Goya* caused little comment at the time. Germany had become accustomed to catastrophe. It was, however, faithfully reported to the Führer Naval Conference on April 18th, the last conference of which there is any record in German archives, for Hitler had only twelve days to live.

The report said:

In connection with the loss of several hundred persons in the sinking of the steamship *Goya*, the C-in-C, Navy, points out that personnel losses in the transports in the Eastern areas up to this time have been extremely small, i.e.

0.49 per cent. These unfortunate losses seem very large every time a ship is sunk, and it is easy to forget that at the same time a large number of ships with numerous wounded and refugees aboard reach port safely.

This was true. Between May 1st and May 8th, small craft ferried 150,000 survivors from the beaches to Hela. From there transports and warships made their perilous runs past the Stolpe Bank. On May 3rd two transports escorted by two torpedo boats, all heavily loaded with troops and refugees, sailed out of Hela. One of the warships was the T 36. It was her last voyage. The next day she was hit by bombs off Swinemunde and then she ran on a mine and sank. She and her Captain, Lieutenant Commander Robert Hering, had had a short but hard war. They had behaved heroically when the *Gustloff* was sunk. They had outwitted Konovalov in the L 3. And they had sailed continuously on convoy escort missions from January 23rd when the evacuation began.

During that time the German Navy and Merchant Navy, using everything from trawlers to liners, had transported nearly a million and a half civilian refugees to the West.

The last convoy to leave sailed on May 8th, the day the war ended, from Libau, the most easterly of the beleaguered ports which had for so long served the German divisions fighting to the end in Courland. The convoy consisted of sixty-five small craft in four groups. It carried nearly 15,000 men.

The next day Soviet ships caught up with the slowest of them and captured 300 men. It was an act which marked the start of a new era. The men who escaped went home to help build West Germany into the most powerful economic nation in Europe, while those who were captured were sent to the labour camps in Russia to help rebuild the Soviet Union.

29

ON APRIL 20TH, 1945, the headquarters of Russia's Baltic Fleet issued a list of orders and medals awarded to members of the fleet for their bravery in action during the first three months of the year.

The S 13, still tied up in Turku harbour at the end of its long patrol, was given a collective award, becoming a "Red Banner" boat. This was a considerable honour and the S 13 was only the second submarine in the division to have its achievements so recognised.

But Marinesko was disappointed. He felt the S 13 ought to have joined the ranks of the élite and become a "Red Guard" ship, a distinction achieved by only sixteen submarines throughout the war.

Every member of the crew got one or other of the two classes of the Order of the Great Patriotic War, of which millions were issued during the war. Marinesko was not satisfied. He felt he deserved to be a Hero of the Soviet Union. But the five-pointed gold star with its red ribbon, worn above all other decorations, was withheld from him. He was not even given the second Order of Lenin, but had to make do with another Order of the Red Banner. A quarter of a million of these medals, embellished with red star, hammer and sickle, and bearing the admonition "Workers of All Countries, Unite!" were dished out during the war. In British terms: "They came up with the rations." To be made a Hero of the Soviet Union was a very different matter. It was an honour of which only 11,600 were judged worthy.

There was also an omission from the citations which infuriated Marinesko: there was no reference in any of them to the sinking of the *Wilhelm Gustloff* or the *General Steuben*.

This was a clear indication that the Military Council did not fully accept that they had been sunk by the S 13.

As Marinesko never tired of telling his superiors, he had sunk Fascist ships totalling 52,144 tons. It was a record. And he had sent at least 10,000 Fascists – the equivalent of a whole division – to the bottom of the sea. And that was another record.

But he was not listened to, and his cup of bitterness ran over when he learned that Captain Vladimir Konovalov had been made a "Hero" for sinking the *Goya*.

Konovalov was one of only six submariners and 600 sailors to win this decoration, and he certainly deserved it. He was credited with sinking ten enemy ships, more than any other commander; and even though the tonnage of four of them is not recorded – which suggests they could have been as small as fishing smacks – and even though the *Goya* was only 5,600 tons, he had nonetheless been in action continuously since 1941. Steady and reliable, he had undertaken more war patrols than his mercurial rival.

At this time, when the war was just coming to an end, Marinesko had little to do. His boat had spent six weeks being refitted and made seaworthy again. But submarine headquarters at Kronstadt seemed in no hurry to send him to sea. He spent his time brooding, drinking, quarrelling with anyone who slighted his submarine. He also spent a lot of time writing a long report of his last patrol based on his log book. Captain Oryel later sent this report to Kronstadt. He also began work on a more ambitious project, a thesis entitled *An Analysis of Torpedo Attacks by the S 13*. He envisaged this becoming the standard textbook on submarine warfare for the Soviet Fleet.

There was no false modesty about Marinesko. He felt he was justified in offering advice on how to handle an attack because of his experience and successes. He believed he had more bodies to his credit than any other Soviet submarine commander, and as soon as headquarters officially confirmed his kills the rest of the navy would know this too. He was the ace. He was convinced that he had something to say which was worth imparting.

He wrote his book out laboriously in longhand, describing in detail his methods of attack and the strengths and weaknesses of the S class submarines. He also criticised the technical deficiencies and the tactical backwardness of the Russian submarine service.

There was indeed much to criticise. Independent naval experts have written of inadequate torpedoes, crude hydrophone devices, and noisy engines. In fact Soviet submariners fought bravely and tenaciously with poor equipment. Their command structure and rules of tactics were also outdated and cumbersome. Marinesko especially criticised the failure of the Air Force to perfect reconnaissance techniques and to lead submarines to targets. He also attacked the outmoded method of employing single submarines operating in sharply defined grid squares, for this method restricted the submarines. They could only lie in ambush, not go hunting. Marinesko wanted more freedom to hunt, especially in co-ordination with the Air Force and other submarines.

This seems a sound exposition of modern warfare. But when Marinesko showed it to several of his colleagues before submitting it to Captain Oryel, they quite rightly warned him that he would be playing into his enemies' hands. They told him that his comments on equipment, tactics and command structure would not be welcomed at staff level and that he would once again be unpopular in high places. They pointed out that there would inevitably be repercussions because he was in effect criticising the naval leadership and the Red Air Force.

Middle-rank officers in services less touchy than those of the USSR might have reconsidered the wisdom of submitting such a thesis in the light of friendly warnings – especially as a new wave of arrests and executions was in full swing. Now that Russia no longer needed the patriotic courage of all those who had fought so bravely against the Germans, Stalin and his secret police were busy rounding up anybody who smelt of dissension.

But Marinesko ignored the warnings, and, as his friends feared, his thesis provided ammunition for those who were envious of his success – and especially for those secret policemen with long memories who would not forget or forgive the way in which he had escaped them after his lost weekend at Turku.

The thesis was never published and it is not known what happened to it. The only trace of it we unearthed was at the submarine training school in Kronstadt where the professional submariners used parts of it in their lectures.

Marinesko made one last patrol with the S 13. He was ordered to sea at the beginning of May 1945. But on May 8th Hitler's once all-powerful war machine whimpered to a halt, and on May 9th Moscow saluted the Russian Armed Forces with thirty salvoes from 1,000 guns. It was Victory Day.

Sasha Marinesko and his crew heard about the end of the war when they surfaced off Bornholm Island to recharge their batteries. The ice of winter had melted, it was a pleasant spring evening, the promise of summer was borne on the breeze off the island and the S 13 celebrated the end of the war with vodka and smoked sausage.

For them there would be no more agonised creeping through the minefields in sweat and fear, no more lying still on the all too shallow bed of the Baltic while the depth charges exploded round them, no more running the gauntlet of the German artillery along the Gulf of Finland, no more manoeuvring to attack and waiting for the crash of their torpedoes against the side of a German ship. It was all over.

But Marinesko remained at sea until he had completed his patrol – for Stalin suspected his allies' intentions and kept his forces on the alert. Accordingly the S 13 returned to Kronstadt on May 24th, the night of the Grand Banquet in the Kremlin when the first toast was to the Soviet fighting men.

A month later a massive two-hour victory parade was held

in Moscow. The T 34s which defeated the Wehrmacht's Panzers rolled through Red Square, followed by massed contingents of the Army and Navy while scores of warplanes led by Stalin's semi-literate, alcoholic son Vassily roared overhead.

No members of the crew of the S 13 were invited to Moscow to take part in the parade. None of them particularly minded. They had had enough. All they wanted now was to go home.

All, that is, except Marinesko. He had become obsessed with his struggle to force the Soviet Navy to acknowledge that the S 13 had sunk the *Wilhelm Gustloff* and the *General Steuben* and to admit that this was a feat which reflected glory on the crew, the division, and the Baltic Fleet as a whole. He complained to his friends that this was the hardest battle of his life.

It took him fifteen years to win. It made him enemies and it cost him friends. He badgered staff officers to review the April 20th awards, and he bored those around him with his complaints of injustice.

"The war is over, Sasha," they told him. At first they were gentle with him and then they lost patience. "Forget about the *Wilhelm Gustloff*," they begged him. But he was obsessed.

Admiral Nikolai Kuznetsov put the story into perspective some twenty-five years later. In an article that appeared in a Leningrad literary journal, Kuznetsov praised the S 13 for its achievements. But he insisted that, although he was Commissar of the Navy, he knew nothing about the sinking of the *Wilhelm Gustloff* until the first week in March. He went on to make the point that at the Yalta Conference in early February, when Churchill urged Stalin to seize the Danzig ports as quickly as possible in order to neutralise the German U-boat threat, nothing was said about the death of the German submariners who were travelling on the liner.

Kuznetsov argued that had Stalin or anyone else on the Stavka (the State Defence Committee) been aware of the killing of the German submariners it would most certainly have been mentioned in this context. In his view they were not aware of it. He explained:

It has to be faced that our armed forces were achieving victory after victory. Hardly a day went by without an artillery salute to honour the liberation of a capital or a city or a town, the crossing of an important river, the defeat of a large enemy group, the capture of a road or railway junction. The roar of the guns and the crack of the multi-coloured rockets which accompanied every volley – sometimes as many as twenty-four – drowned out the sound of the S 13's torpedoes sinking Fascist ships.

Admiral Kuznetsov also insisted that not only was the report in the *Stockholm Tidningen* the only "confirmation" of the sinking but it was not seen in Moscow until after the war. He pointed out that the Soviet Air Force had been active in the Danzig Bay at the same time as Marinesko and so the liner could have been sunk by aircraft – or at least, that is what it might have looked like to some officers.

He explained that in early April the general staff considered a recommendation to award Marinesko his coveted title of Hero of the Soviet Union, but rejected the idea. This was a considered decision, not an accidental omission. There were "people who pointed out Marinesko's many deficiencies and weaknesses and who recalled that one day he could perform a heroic deed but the next he could be late returning to his ship or in the some other way violate military discipline".

There were other voices being raised against Marinesko. Jealous of his popularity, some of his brother officers were insisting that he was "lucky" and that the two ships had simply presented themselves as sitting targets to him. They argued that any other averagely competent submariner with the normal amount of courage would also have taken on the two ships and made off under cover of darkness.

Kuznetsov rejected this line as diplomatically as he could. He agreed that any other Soviet commander would have done the same thing given the opportunity, but said that Marinesko had sought out the enemy, handled the S 13 brilliantly to get into an attack position, and when hunted and depth-charged made the right decisions to bring the submarine and his crew to safety.

The Admiral himself was to experience a buffeting in his career. After the war he was twice demoted from his high position as First Deputy Minister of Defence as well as that of Naval Commander in Chief. Finally, with the rank of Vice Admiral, he was given a minor job in the central apparatus of the Ministry of Defence.

In his memoirs Khrushchev wrote of the downfall of Kuznetsov and of how the Presidium rejected the Admiral's plans for a significant and costly build-up of the surface navy. "I could see Kuznetsov was boiling with hatred. From that day on he began expressing himself openly not only against the decision we'd made but against our leadership. He began demonstrating with us, displaying openly his obstinacy and arrogance . . ."

Those words could equally have been applied to Alexander Marinesko as he clashed with his superiors in the summer of 1945.

In September 1945 the "attack ace" was relieved of his command of the S 13 and offered the command of a mine-sweeper. Enraged and drunk, he refused to take over the ship and was promptly demoted two ranks to First Lieutenant. His enemies went to work on the "Odessa street urchin", and the NKGB file on his escapade in Turku was circulated. In October he was dismissed from the Soviet Navy for an "indifferent and casual attitude to the service".

Marinesko, shaken but not demoralised by this blow, tried to fight back. He applied to join the Soviet Merchant Fleet – which is part of the Navy – thinking that his experience and background would be welcome. It was belatedly discovered that he was slightly shortsighted in one eye. Normally this defect would not have prevented him from being in the Navy or even from commanding a warship. It had certainly not prevented him from sinking the *Wilhelm Gustloff*. But once again the NKGB file was taken out of the cabinet. Marinesko was unreliable. Perhaps it was unwise to allow him to hold a job where he might travel to foreign ports.

In January 1946, aged thirty-three, former submarine commander Alexander Marinesko, holder of the Order of Lenin, two Orders of the Red Banner and several victory and campaign medals, went ashore and found a job as a storeman in an organisation dealing in building materials in Leningrad.

30

ACCORDING TO VLADIMIR DMITRIYEV, author of *Submarines Attack*:

Having left the Navy soon after the war, Marinesko returned to his peacetime profession [that is, the Merchant Navy]. In the postwar years, as Captain of the Soviet steamers *Yalta* and *Sever*, he sailed many seas and oceans. But the war had taken its toll. The right eye of the Captain got worse and worse and in 1950 Marinesko decided to go ashore. The former Baltic submariner was warmly received into the collective of one of the Leningrad factories.

But this was not true. Marinesko was not readmitted to the Merchant Navy. He commanded neither the *Yalta* nor the *Sever*. And by 1950 he was already in Siberia.

Leningrad had been besieged for 900 days by the Germans, who came within seven kilometres of the city centre. The blockade killed 600,000 people through bombing, shelling, disease and starvation. The survivors made loaves out of the sawdust on the bakery floors and at times some of them ate the bodies of their dead relatives. The city was shattered. Life was hard and drab after the war. Goods and food were desperately short and a black market flourished in every commodity. Bribery and corruption became a way of life, for where there has been near-cannibalism, other "crimes of survival" seem petty.

The boy from Odessa who had spent his early life rubbing shoulders with crooks of every kind should have been in his element. Bruised and bitter by being dismissed from the Navy, failing to find a job at sea, and drinking heavily, he could almost have been forgiven if he had joined the corrupt officials and speculators. He did not do so.

It did not take him long to discover that he was working for a state construction trust where the director and many of the workers were taking bribes for delivering materials to party officials building private dachas (villas) outside Leningrad. Marinesko could have kept his mouth shut. Instead he made it known that he disapproved of what was going on – "we didn't fight the Fascists for this sort of thing" – and wanted no part of it. And the director waited for him to make a false move.

Much of what happened thereafter is obscure, and the authorities in Leningrad are reluctant to open their legal files for what they contemptuously dismiss as a minor case. And certainly, by the standards of the time, it *was* a minor case. But it was enough to take a large slice out of Marinesko's life.

He fell into the trap through generosity. Noticing several tons of damaged and discarded building blocks and bricks in the yard of the enterprise, he suggested to the director that instead of being dumped they should be given away to workers of the trust as New Year gifts. Marinesko supervised the delivery of the broken blocks and refused offers of money for them.

But informers are a part of life in the Soviet Union and it took only a few weeks for one of them to tell the police about the blocks. Enquiries led to the construction trust and Marinesko. The director denied that he had given permission for the rubble to leave the yard. Marinesko was arrested and charged with stealing the property of the State. At that time the theft of building materials was widespread and hard to control, and officials and the police were usually only half-hearted in their efforts to stamp it out. For a while, therefore, it looked as though Marinesko was going to escape punishment except for the loss of his Communist Party card.

But he was made to stand trial in a People's Court in Leningrad. The Prosecutor, a former naval officer, appreciated that he had committed no crime and that the case should never have been brought. He asked for Marinesko to be acquitted – a most unusual procedure in a Russian court. The judge's two assistants agreed but the judge did not. He ordered that Marinesko should be kept in prison and retried.

From then on the former commander of the S 13 stood no chance of escape. He was dealt with by a Special Board, a quasi-judicial body of three NKGB officers, otherwise known as a "Troika", which concentrated on "political" crimes and specialised in finding labour for the camps. They pronounced him guilty. The sentence was three years, in itself a modest term. The terror of it lay in the place where he was to serve it. He was to go to Kolyma. Just one island in Solzhenitsyn's *Gulag Archipelago*, the Kolyma region was the most infamous of the huge labour-camp complex.

In his book *Kolyma, the Arctic Death Camps*, Robert Conquest writes:

Basically the frightfulness of Kolyma was due not to geographical or climate reasons, but to conscious decisions taken in Moscow. For a few years before 1937, in fact, it was well administered and the death rate was low. The climate, though exceedingly cold, is a remarkably healthy one for men who are properly fed, clothed and sheltered. In this earlier phase, the main aim of the administration was to produce gold efficiently. In the later period (as one commandant put it quite openly) though the gold remained important, the central aim was to kill off the prisoners. In the earliest period of the labour camp system, the Solovki camps on the islands of the White Sea were the symbol of the whole system, the worst killers. These were followed in the mid-thirties by the camps of the Baltic-White Sea canal. Kolyma took their place just when the system was reaching its maximum expansion, and remained central to it for the next fifteen years, as (in Solzhenitsyn's words) "the pole of cold and cruelty" of the labour camp system.

Marinesko would have learnt about Kolyma in Leningrad's Kresty prison and realised that his chances of being released after three years were remote. The Gulag does not give up its victims so easily. All he could hope for was to survive the marathon journey to the far east of Russia, insist on being treated as "non-political", and land a cosy job. Perhaps as he prepared himself he thought of the convict's song of his youth: "Goodbye, my Odessa, Sweet Quarantine.* Tomorrow we're off to Far Sakhalin . . ."

It is not known what part Marinesko's secret police file played in this sentence, but his judges would certainly have had it before them when they decided to send him to Siberia, a fate sufficient to crush even the bravest spirit.

Prisoners were transported to Siberia in railway wagons named after Stolypin, the Tsarist official whose repression of the 1905 revolution filled earlier railway carriages going east. The "Stolypin" carriage is an ordinary passenger car divided into compartments but without windows, so that it looks like a baggage car. The prisoners occupy five of the nine compartments and their guards the rest. The prisoners' compartments are open to the corridors, but barred off by gratings. Solzhenitsyn in a memorable description wrote: "From the corridor side all this is very reminiscent of a menagerie: pitiful creatures resembling human beings are huddled there in cages, the floors and bunks surrounded on all sides by metal grilles, looking out at you pitifully, begging for something to eat and drink, except that in menageries they never crowd the wild animals in so tightly."

He went on to describe how one man travelled for three weeks in a compartment that started out with thirty-six people in it. "For several days he hung suspended between other human beings and his legs did not touch the floor. They started to die off – and the guards hauled the corpses out from

* Quarantine was the main pier at Odessa harbour. It took its name from the maritime medical station.

under their feet . . . That way things became less crowded." That was in the autumn of 1946.

Marinesko's 6,000-mile journey from Leningrad along the Trans-Siberian Railway probably began in 1947 and took several months. Apart from the authority-inflicted hardships of the journey there were dangers to be faced from the hardened criminals, the murderers and rapists, who bullied and stole from those whom they regarded as vulnerable – the "politicals" sentenced for anti-Soviet activity under the catch-all Article 58.

The "Blatnye", the companionship of thieves, thrived in the Gulag and they were encouraged by the guards to rob and bully the politicals. In Marinesko's carriage there was just such a group, run by a thug who had been given twenty-five years for helping German punishment squads to round up civilians. It was he whom the guards made boss of the carriage and to whom they gave the choice job of doling out the food rations.

Marinesko later told friends that this man and a small group of toughs "began to terrorise the rest of us", and went on to explain what he had done about it. "This bastard and his cronies gave themselves two mugfuls of soup and everyone else only one, and then it wasn't even a full mug. I soon realised that I was not going to see the Pacific Ocean at this rate and that I had to do something about it.

"There were eight of us sailors in that *Vagzek* [prisoner's wagon] and they didn't take much organising. When the soup came round and the bastards started issuing it I gave the signal and we went for them. We gave the Fascist-lover such a beating we nearly killed him. Certainly we shut him up. Then I appointed as wagon boss a lad who had got a fiver for stealing a tin of meat while unloading a ship. The convoy chief was satisfied that we were not planning to escape and ignored what had happened. So we made it to Vladivostok."

It was not journey's end. From Nakhodka and Vanino, near Khabarovsk, the prison ships sailed north to the splendid harbour at Nagayevo, the port for Kolyma, the gateway to the death camps.

Tens of thousands of starved, sick, humiliated men and women were driven in columns to the floating dungeons. There, as the dissident Roy Medvedev wrote in his *Let History Judge*, people often lay on top of each other in the crowded holds "and bread was thrown to them through the hatches as if they were beasts. Those who died during the voyage – and they were many – were simply thrown into the sea. A riot or an organised protest was met with icy water, poured into the hold from the Sea of Okhotsk. Thousands of prisoners died after such a bath, or were delivered frostbitten to the hospitals of Magadan." Rape was another feature of the journey. The women prisoners were used by the guards and the criminals alike, while those wives who followed their husbands to the camps were forced into prostitution in order to survive.

Once the prisoners reached Nagayevo they were marched away to the 125 camps from which many of them never emerged.

It took twenty or thirty days to turn a healthy man into a wreck. According to the writer V. T. Shalamov, a veteran of the Kolyma camps: "Working in the camp mine sixteen hours a day, without any days off, with systematic starvation, ragged clothes, sleeping in a torn tent at sixty below zero, did the job. Beatings by the foremen, by the ringleaders of the thieves, by the guards, speeded up the process . . ."

Medvedev records that over the gates of all the camps in the Kolyma region was the inscription required by the camp statute: "Labour is a matter of honour, valour and heroism."

This was the place that Marinesko, submarine ace of the Baltic Fleet, had reached. But his wits had not deserted him. The slave ships, three of which were built on Teesside before the war, also carried supplies for the mines and the camps and they needed to be unloaded and then loaded again with the Gulag's products for the return voyage to Vladivostok.

Marinesko knew about loading ships. He was fit, and he

was not a "political". So why not become a trusty? Why go and die in the mines like some three million others? He persuaded the authorities that he and the eight sailors would make a formidable brigade of dockers.

The name of the game was the same as that which he had played in the Baltic: survival.

Two years after Stalin's death in 1953 the camp gates began to open. Millions of prisoners went home to pick up the threads of their lives. Some of the dead were posthumously "rehabilitated". For some of the living there were apologies for "mistakes connected with Stalin's cult of personality".

Marinesko had survived and he was let out to make the long journey back to Leningrad, where he finally went to work in the Leningrad factory about which Dmitriyev wrote, and rejoined the Communist Party. That he was allowed to do so was a sign that he had been forgiven for whatever it was that had earned him banishment to Kolyma.

He had not been forgotten. Even during the darkest days after the war, his friends in the navy had embarked on a quiet campaign to have him released and rehabilitated. Gradually they began to make headway. The breakthrough came in 1960 when a television programme was made about the sinking of the *Gustloff* and he was credited with that feat.

Shortly afterwards he was reinstated in the retired rank of Captain Third Class and awarded the appropriate pension. The Central Naval Museum in Leningrad gave him credit for his achievements.

This museum, once the Stock Exchange of St. Petersburg, now houses some 200,000 exhibits, and in Hall No. 8, devoted to "The Victory Over Fascism in East Prussia, 1945", there is a case containing a photograph of Alexander Ivanovitch Marinesko and his six medals, the Order of Lenin, two Orders of the Red Banner, two Patriotic War Medals, First and Second Class, and the Leningrad Victory Medal.

Visitors learn that A. I. Marinesko commanded the S 13 between 1943 and 1945; that the submarine sank three enemy transport ships; that on January 30th, 1945, the S 13 attacked the German Fascist liner *Wilhelm Gustloff* of more than 25,000 tons. Three torpedoes, the text in the museum goes on, were on target and the enemy ship was sunk. On board the liner, which the Hitlerites were using for the evacuation of Danzig, were several thousand soldiers, sailors and officers. There were also a number of submariners.

To confirm the account there is a photograph of a cutting from a Swedish newspaper. Neither the name of the newspaper (*Stockholm Tidningen*) nor the date of its publication is shown. The Swedish is translated into Russian and reads:

> According to reports in the morning newspapers the German ship *Wilhelm Gustloff*, 20,000 tons, was torpedoed and sunk on Thursday soon after it left Danzig. Of the 8,000 people on board only 988 were saved. There were 3,700 specialist submariners on the ship who would have taken part in the war. And 3,000 refugees from the East. The liner began to sink ten minutes after the torpedoes struck and went down in five minutes.

This was belated recognition. For though now Marinesko stood in the company of his peers, with the portraits of other Soviet submarine heroes flanking his on the same wall, for fifteen years – until the summer of 1960 – he had been an "unperson". His name and exploits were never mentioned in the Soviet press. The museum itself was almost equally uninformative. For all that visitors could tell, Marinesko did not exist and the sinking of the two German ships had not occurred. The sole – and oblique – reference to the submarine's presence was an oil painting showing the S 13 battling through rough seas with a German ship in the background. It hung high on a wall and was untitled. Only if pressed would museum officials make available the submarine's war record and the name of its commander.

It took the efforts and courage of two Soviet writers,

Alexander Kron and Sergei Smirnov, and the support of two Admirals, Ivan Isakov and Nikolai Kuznetsov, to get the former war hero rehabilitated, his rank restored, his pension increased, his place on the wall of the museum secured.

Finally, in October 1963, at the annual reunion of the Baltic submariners at Kronstadt, his friends performed the ceremony of the roast sucking pig in his honour. They stood and applauded him. At last he was vindicated.

But it was eighteen years too late. Within three weeks, he was dead of cancer.

31

AT MIDNIGHT ON May 8th–9th, 1945, the war in the West ended. In its final stages the Baltic, the very area where it had all begun when the Nazi armies moved into Poland in 1939, again became the key theatre of operations.

The evacuation across the East Sea, as the Germans call the Baltic, was the last operation of the Third Reich. There is a special poignancy about the last battle of a great war, and about the deaths of men and women on the eve of peace. The question springs to mind: why should so many thousands have died aboard the *Wilhelm Gustloff*, and the other stricken ships in those cold northern seas, when peace was at hand? Was anything achieved by the final operations on sea and land which brought so much pain and suffering?

To discover the answer it is necessary to consider what happened in Europe once the war ended, and in particular to take account of the rebuilding of West Germany and its integration into a new Europe welded together in the post-war years under threatening pressure from the Soviet Union. It is also illuminating to study the views of surviving statesmen from that period as they look back in tranquillity.

It is the proud contention of Gross Admiral Karl Doenitz that the actions he took at that time were of incalculable value. He believes that he played an important part in laying the foundations of post-war Germany.

Between January 23rd and May 8th, 1945 [he wrote in his memoirs], 2,022,602 persons from Courland, East and West Prussia, and later from Pomerania and parts of Mecklenburg, were safely transported by sea to the West. The evacuations had been carried out under constant

187

attack by British, American and Russian aircraft, by Russian submarines and light coastal forces, and through waters repeatedly and heavily mined. The losses that occurred were truly appalling – 4,000 were lost with the *Wilhelm Gustloff*,* 7,000 with the *Goya* and 3,000 with the hospital ship *Steuben*. Painful though these losses were, they represented only one per cent of the total brought out by sea; ninety-nine per cent succeeded in arriving safely at ports on the western Baltic.

When one of the authors visited Admiral Doenitz in June 1978, this remarkable man, then an alert eighty-seven, made it clear that he looked back on his success in negotiating the capitulation of Nazi Germany as the greatest achievement of his career.

Stiff and frail, he proved a stickler for protocol. He received Ronald Payne at his villa at Aumuhle, a comfortable country establishment close to Hamburg and not far from the River Elbe, and devoted several minutes to organising the seating arrangements for those present in his book-lined living room.

He himself was to sit on a sofa in front of a long, low coffee table. Opposite him, in a formal row, he placed Captain Reitsch, a retired naval officer who acts as his ADC; Frau Reitsch, his wife, who, as we have recorded, commanded the Women Auxiliaries in Gdynia; and Christian Wieg, the young interpreter. Payne's chair was at the end of the table, on Reitsch's left and the Admiral's right.

"Are you a Britisher or German?" the Admiral enquired of Wieg, as he completed this *placement*.

"German – *Deutscher*."

"What nationality?" asked the Admiral, who is rather deaf and finds strange voices difficult.

"*Deutscher Abiturient*," bellowed Captain Reitsch in his best quarterdeck voice.

---

* Authors' note: As already stated, our researches have led us to the conclusion that the losses were much higher.

Only then did the Admiral sit down, straight-backed and looking very formal in his dark grey suit, white shirt and smart striped tie. The housekeeper, who was clearly in charge of the rather cluttered salon, had already placed a silver tray by his elbow. It bore a bottle of spa water, some good English sherry, and a number of silver goblets. The old man insisted on superintending the distribution of goblets and then sipped some mineral water.

"I wish to speak with Herr Payne in English," he said. "I have not spoken English for twenty years, but I wish to help him."

He spoke slowly and correctly, articulating carefully, in a high-pitched, slightly tremulous, but authoritative voice, and cautiously recalled the momentous events in which he had been so closely involved thirty-three years before. It was noticeable that he hesitated when mentioning his attempts to make a separate peace with the British and the Americans, and seemed reluctant to use the phrase "German capitulation", even when his friends, the Reitsches, prompted him.

The Admiral clutched various documents from a thick folder, and to refresh his memory pulled out a few sheets of wartime paper on which statistics were typed. The point he was most anxious to make concerned the importance of his success in rescuing from the Russians so many of his fellow countrymen and women at a time when it was obvious that Nazi Germany had been defeated and was rapidly falling into chaos.

"It is most important," he declared. "In December 1944, it was quite clear to me that the main task for the German Navy was not any longer the U-boat Krieg. Time was too short for that. All the naval force we had was to be assembled to save the people from the East and bring them back West.

"That is why I asked the State, in other words, Hitler, to give me every German merchant ship that could be found, everything that floated. I did that in order to save people from the East. I commandeered oil and fuel for transport. I was given complete power throughout the north of Germany, and decided what should be done with fuel supplies."

It was natural that Admiral Doenitz should be so moved by the plight of people in the East being overrun by the Red Army, and so conscious that the state needed them. He had been born in Berlin, the descendant of a long line of Prussians who served the state as officers or Lutheran pastors. A small, compact man, in appearance he is far removed from the caricature picture of a Prussian officer. But he was reared in the Prussian tradition of self-sacrifice and obedience.

At the age of nineteen, a boy with high cheekbones and a long upturned nose, he entered the navy in 1910 and served in cruisers of the Kaiser's fleet before transferring to the newly formed submarine service.

In 1915 his damaged submarine U 68 surfaced among British destroyers in the Mediterranean off Sicily, and he was taken prisoner of war. He survived the remainder of the war without further adventures and joined the new navy in 1919. After 1933 he gave his support to Hitler and achieved rapid promotion. He said at Nuremberg:

"Naturally I admired and joyfully recognised the high authority of Adolf Hitler because he succeeded in realising the national and social aims without spilling blood."

In the course of the Second World War Admiral Doenitz grew closer to Hitler, serving him faithfully as commander of the U-boat flotillas. But, by the beginning of 1945, while still doing all he could to keep his submarine force in action, he realised that Hitler's war machine was now damaged beyond repair and that the vital remaining task was the evacuation of Germans across the Baltic.

What finally decided him was when a copy of "Eclipse", a British operations order containing plans and measures to be taken when the Allies occupied Germany after unconditional surrender, fell into German hands in January 1945. A map attached to it delineated the proposed zones of occupation by Americans. British and Russians. It would, he wrote later, "put an end to our existence as a corporate national entity".

Discovery of the plan stiffened resistance among the German leadership to any idea of ending the war through negotiation. If the Allies were going to insist on the harsh terms of unconditional surrender, the Third Reich would go down fighting.

To Doenitz it was obvious that capitulation would be followed by an immediate freeze on the movement of German troops, who would be forced to lay down their arms wherever they were and to go into captivity. "Had we capitulated during the winter months of 1944–45, three and a half million soldiers on the Eastern Front – which was then still a long way from the Anglo-American front in the West – would have fallen into the hands of the Russians." His aim, accordingly, was to get troops and refugees back into areas which would eventually be occupied by the Americans or the British.

He wanted an area of safety rather than a laager of resistance. Later, when he took over as Germany's leader after Hitler's death, he also sought to achieve a separate peace with Britain and America.

His first priority was to keep open as long as possible a land escape route to the West along the Baltic coast for troops and refugees in flight before Rokossovsky's Second Byelo-Russian Army. But on May 2nd troops of Field Marshal Montgomery's 21st Army Group thrust across the Elbe and captured Lübeck, thus closing the land gateway with the West. Now that Schleswig-Holstein was in British hands, Doenitz could see no further reason for fighting, and he promptly despatched Admiral von Friedeburg to Montgomery's headquarters to offer to surrender North-West Germany to him.

Montgomery received the emissary coldly, though he saw at once the advantage of a British general officer accepting such a great surrender, and added that the German was "no monster". After a second visit from Friedeburg, and without consulting General Eisenhower, the Supreme Commander, he agreed to accept the surrender of all the German forces in his area under Doenitz's control. "Forces to be surrendered total over a million chaps. Not so bad, a million chaps. Good egg!" he exclaimed, with Monty-ish bounce.

Admiral Doenitz is convinced that this arrangement was of capital importance in his plan to save as many Germans as possible from Russian slavery.

At the interview with Payne in June 1978 he said: "I tried to make peace with England and the United States at the end, but only Montgomery would agree. That gave me two days to stand in the East against the Russians before the Americans signed, and that meant that 1,850,000 soldiers came back, many of them overland. Eisenhower had said, 'No'. It was good that Montgomery made peace with me at once. It saved those people from Russian hands.

"I was surprised that Montgomery told me, 'Yes, I do it'. Churchill was the only man who knew that the situation had changed and realised the need for a stronger Germany to prevent the Russians getting Europe. Churchill wrote one of the best documents of the war. I have it here."

Later, he read out an order from himself issued in the pause between the surrender to Montgomery and that to Eisenhower and the Russians. It commanded the use, up to one minute before midnight, of "every ship, every cruiser, destroyer, torpedo boat, merchant ship, fishing boat and rowing boat", to get more people back across the water to the West. By such means were thousands snatched at the very last moment from the vengeance of the Russian invaders.

This rescue operation of May 1945 had far-reaching effects both for Germany and Western Europe. Without it the post-war German miracle might never have been achieved, for the revival of West Germany needed manpower as well as Marshall Aid and Allied encouragement. It is ironic to reflect that Admiral Doenitz's initial worry was whether Western Germany could house and feed the refugees. In fact, the country had been drained of millions of men, and chaotic, overcrowded and impoverished as it then appeared, it absorbed the newcomers with ease. They in turn helped to create the new German democracy that now stands as a linch-pin of the Common Market and a pillar of Nato.

However, despite the successful efforts of Admiral Doenitz and the German Navy, there were many Germans who stayed in the East, reluctant to leave land their families had farmed for generations. Others, trapped behind the Russian advance, found their means of escape cut off, and of these, the most important for the future were the technicians. A very special group was composed of the scientists and skilled workers who had been busy developing the new German U-boats in the dockyards on the Baltic coast. Many fell into Russian hands at precisely the moment when the Americans were snapping up Wernher von Braun's rocket scientists in the west.

Of the revolutionary new submarines themselves, Churchill wrote with great foresight: "This weapon in Soviet hands lies among the hazards of the future." They had certainly caused great worry to the Admiralty during the last months of the war. Included in the Russian booty when they took over the Baltic yards were four completed type XXI boats and a completed submarine of the even more advanced XXIII type, together with a number of prefabricated sections. At the Schichau shipyard in Danzig there were no less than eight type XXI boats under construction. The Russians promptly set their captured German experts to work and within a short time had at their disposal a modern fleet infinitely more powerful than anything they had possessed before.

With new engines, new breathing devices, and new torpedo controls, these submarines could run faster, deeper, and for longer periods than anything the Allies could operate at the end of the war. From them the Russians developed the powerful Z, Q, and W classes which became the mainstay of the Soviet Fleet at the height of the Cold War. And from these again sprang the constructional and operational know-how for the nuclear-powered ballistic missile under-water fleet which is the foundation of the Kremlin's naval power today.

Even before the Second World War Stalin had insisted on the construction of "the most powerful navy in the world". He always yearned to have the might of a surface and underwater fleet behind him, for he believed that in naval as well as in military strength the cradle of Communism must be able to outmatch the strongest Capitalist nations. In particular, his forces must be bigger and better than those of the Royal Navy.

Until the end of the war the reality lagged behind the dream. Russia lacked the means and knowledge to build the sort of powerful surface ships that Stalin demanded, and the Red Navy's commanders, Orlov, Miklevich and Ludri, concentrated their efforts on light coastal forces and a defensive fleet of submarines. Stalin assumed that his naval chiefs were deliberately opposing his plan, and they all died in his purge of the navy in the 1930s. Their technical arguments were set aside as sabotage, "a crime against the Party".

When war came, they were proved right. Obsolescent, under-gunned, thin-skinned and under-powered, the surface ships on which the Russian dictator had insisted accomplished practically nothing. Their crews were taken away and converted into infantry. Throughout the war no Russian warship larger than an MTB managed to sink any enemy vessel by gunfire.

It was fortunate for the Red Navy that Admiral Lev Galler, appointed to replace his executed brother officers, was a commander of the old school. He had served in the Russian Imperial Navy and bravely insisted that the submarine should be the principal attack weapon against enemy shipping. For his bold stand he paid the price after the war. He was arrested in 1947 on trumped-up charges of giving away the secrets of a parachute torpedo. Three years later he died in prison.

Even the submarines of the Red Fleet had a poor wartime record, bravely commanded and manned though they were; for both in equipment and tactics they were out of date. For a loss of 108 submarines they managed to sink only 108 merchant ships and twenty-eight small warships. In the Baltic, bottled in by minefields and steel nets across the Gulf of Finland, they managed only to sink forty-five ships and lost an equal number of submarines. But three of those ships were the *Wilhelm Gustloff*, the *Steuben* and the *Goya*.

There can be no doubt that the success of Marinesko and others in sinking such giants and killing so many "Fascist lackeys" convinced Stalin of the need to build up a fleet of large ocean-going submarines. As soon as the war ended it again became his ambition to match the power of the most powerful Capitalist navies. But by that time it was the United States Navy that he wished to emulate. With its war-proven carriers, battleships and submarines, it had left the Royal Navy behind. Now America ruled the waves.

But not for long. Today it is the Soviet Navy, with its great fleet of nuclear-powered submarines, armed with rockets targeted on the major cities of the West, that challenges America itself on the high seas.

Both the sons of Vladimir Konovalov, who in his antiquated boat succeeded in sinking the *Goya*, are now captains of nuclear submarines of the Soviet Navy – an indication of the amazing speed with which the Russian fleet has been transformed. Thus they live on to keep their father's fame alive. But except for a diminishing band of his friends, who bravely fought for his rehabilitation as a hero, few Russians now remember Marinesko and his exploits. His career is still a "political" matter, and investigators are still discouraged from enquiring into his career.

Despite that, we believe that Marinesko and Konovalov, who between them sank three great liners, and Admiral Doenitz of the German Navy, who brought two million of his compatriots across the sea, should not be forgotten, for their actions helped to shape our world.

Postscript – Forever Amber

GAULEITER ERICH KOCH was one of the monsters of the Second World War. His first request on being appointed Reich Kommissar of the Ukraine was for Himmler to draft in his Einsatzkommandos (extermination squads). There, and in Poland, his death score numbered hundreds of thousands. He sent old men and beardless boys to their deaths in defence of his domain in East Prussia. And he conspired to have General Lasch sentenced to death for surrendering Königsberg when he himself had already fled the city.

It was April 23rd when this abominable man decided to cut and run. Berlin was surrounded, the Führer Headquarters was no longer in charge of events, and it was obvious that the much-vaunted miracle weapons could not now save Germany. So Koch decided that he had better save himself.

But he resolved to move cautiously. It would be awkward if the Führer should, by some remote chance, survive and learn that the man who had been preaching no surrender had run away.

So he boarded his commandeered icebreaker, *Ostpreussen*, at Pillau only when it seemed that the city must follow Königsberg and fall within hours. And as the ship steamed away he continued to send grandiose messages about the fight he was carrying on. He had installed a powerful radio for this purpose and had manned it with his personal operators. He also had his own gunners for the anti-aircraft weapons mounted on the icebreaker.

But one class of passenger was conspicuously missing. When he gave orders for the *Ostpreussen* to be made ready to sail at 1900 hours on April 23rd with his Mercedes, his dogs and ample supplies of food and drink on board, Koch also instructed the Captain that under no circumstances was he to take on board any refugees or wounded soldiers.

Pillau was in flames, pounded by Russian artillery and bombers; and refugees were scrambling aboard anything that would float as the weary, beaten soldiers of the Wehrmacht manned their last positions to give the civilians time to get away. But such was Koch's inhumanity that when the officers from his staff went on board the icebreaker with his final orders before sailing, they were instructed to tell the first engineer that he must put ashore his own wife and family. Koch reaffirmed these orders when he arrived. Only when the ship's officers refused to take the ship out without the engineer's family did the Gauleiter back down. In other times he would have had them all shot. Now he needed them to save his skin.

He boarded the icebreaker at 1800 hours and sailed for Hela accompanied by his reserve ship, the *Pregel*. They arrived as the crowded peninsula was once again being attacked from the air. Koch made his way to the port commander who was striving to get all the refugees away and demanded a special naval escort, claiming that he had to carry out an important mission for the Führer. But the navy would have none of it. They told him to join a convoy and suggested that no doubt he had space on the *Ostpreussen* for some refugees as well. They were right. There was room for four hundred.

Full of bluster and threats, Koch returned to the ship, even refusing to take on board survivors of his own People's Army. He claimed that the *Ostpreussen* was needed for more military duties. Stripping the *Pregel* of all her fuel he sailed off on his own.

As they pushed westwards, Koch continued to broadcast messages to Hitler in which he claimed to be carrying on the fight. He stopped only when his radio brought him the news that the Battle for Berlin was almost over and that both Goering and Himmler had attempted to open negotiations with the Western Allies and had been expelled from their positions by Hitler.

The *Ostpreussen* would have made an ideal target for Marinesko or Konovalov as she made her way along the Pomeranian coast. And there were men on board her who deserved the terrible death which the Soviet submariners had inflicted on the wounded soldiers and refugees of the *Gustloff*, *Steuben* and *Goya*. But such are the fortunes of war. The innocent died, while Koch and his unsavoury cronies sailed westwards, first to Sassnitz on the island of Rugen, where they were refused entry to the harbour because it was being turned into a last ditch fortress; then – to avoid the mines sown by the RAF – to the island of Bornholm; and then along the Swedish coast to Copenhagen.

Hitler committed suicide on April 30th and the boatload of Nazis accepted that that was the end; they had been defeated. They began to drink from the copious stock of looted liquor that Koch had stored on board. But in the midst of these scenes of "eat, drink and be merry" they began to make their preparations to escape the retribution which they knew would follow. Party uniforms were·dumped overboard. Civilian clothes were taken out of suitcases. Some SS officers and Nazi officials assumed the identity of ordinary soldiers.

They did not stop long in Copenhagen, where the Danish resistance was in evidence, but sailed on to arrive at Flensburg on May 7th. Flensburg was the new seat of government of the crumbling Third Reich. Doenitz had taken over as President and Supreme Commander from the dead Hitler and had made his headquarters at the port, which was naval territory. Albert Speer writes in *Inside the Third Reich*: "The Gross Admiral said no to any plan to transfer himself and the new government to Denmark or Prague, despite the fact that Flensburg might be occupied by the British any day. Himmler in particular felt drawn to Prague. An old imperial city, he urged, was more fitting as the headquarters of a government than historically insignificant Flensburg.

"He omitted to add that by moving to Prague we would be passing from the sphere where the navy held power into the sphere of the SS. Doenitz finally cut off the discussion by stating flatly that we would certainly not continue our activities beyond the German borders. 'If the British want to capture us here, let them do it.' "

This refusal by Doenitz to pass under the control of the SS did not suit Koch. Arriving at Flensburg he went to the Gross Admiral and demanded a U-boat to take him to South America. Doenitz refused, and Koch disappeared. Assuming the identity of Major Rolf Berger of the Army Reserve, he drove away and did not surface again until 1949. Then he was recognised by a British officer and arrested on a farm near Hamburg where he had been working as a labourer. In his trouser pocket he had a capsule of potassium cyanide, similar to those which were issued to the leading Nazis towards the end of the war and which several of them, including Himmler and Goering, finally swallowed. Koch did not swallow his.

Both the Russians and the Poles wished to lay their hands on Koch. The Russians wanted him for the series of massacres carried out during his régime as Commissioner for the Ukraine. In Kiev alone 195,000 people were exterminated between September 1941, when he took over, and May 1943, when he fled before the advancing Russian Army. He deported thousands of Russians as slave labourers and in the province of Rovno, where he had his headquarters, gas wagons were used to kill 102,000 people, many of them Jews, for Koch was a virulent anti-Semite.

Demanding his extradition, the Russians said that he was the "number one war criminal in the Ukraine", and when he appeared before a British extradition tribunal in November 1949 it was shown that even his colleagues among the Nazi leaders had protested against his cruelty.

A letter to Himmler from Reichsminister Alfred Rosenberg, head of the Ministry for Occupied Eastern Territories, was produced by the prosecution. In it, Rosenberg complained about Koch's activities in the Ukraine and accused him of killing more than 200 small landowners in order to provide himself with a shooting estate.

This was the sort of insane behaviour that lost the war for Hitler, for when the Germans first advanced into the Ukraine they were met with flowers and greeted as liberators from a hated régime. If the Germans had exploited this good will, treated the Ukrainians generously and won their cooperation, the result might have been the break-up of the Soviet Union. But Koch and his party colleagues soon showed themselves even more barbaric than the Communists and let the opportunity slip through their bloody hands, much to the disgust of more far-sighted men, such as the Intelligence chief, General Reinhard Gehlen, who was working to turn the Russian people against Communism.

Because of a time limit on extradition to Russia for war crimes, Koch was handed over to the Poles who, for some reason still unexplained, did not put him on trial for another eight years. He was accused of the murder of 72,000 Poles, including 10,000 children, and of more than 200,000 Jews. He was obviously ill when his trial opened in 1958 and the *Daily Telegraph* Special Correspondent described the scene:

> The former Gauleiter, who but for his having remained in hiding for three and a half years would have faced trial together with other Nazi leaders at Nuremberg, cut a sorry figure indeed when he was half-carried, half-dragged, into the court room by two uniformed militia men and slumped in his chair throughout the hearing. A prison hospital nurse and two doctors sat in attendance.

But ill as he was, Koch still retained his instinct for survival.

He spoke in his own defence whenever an opportunity presented itself and even challenged the prosecutor on points of detail. He asked for the court to be adjourned to examine his physical condition, which he attributed to maltreatment, and strongly denied suggestions that he was shamming. He declared that since his transfer from prison hospital to the Mokotow prison in Warsaw, his life had been made a "living hell" by other prisoners, mostly petty criminals, and that he had twice been assaulted. "Free me from the hell in which I live and send me to a hospital where I can become fit enough to render proper account for that of which I am accused before the Polish people, whom I have learnt to honour and revere," he unctuously declaimed.

He got short shrift from State Prosecutor Smolenske, who said that the authorities did not tolerate, approve or inspire the sort of treatment complained about but that obviously the criminals disliked him as much as did everyone else. He suggested that Koch's demand was merely a ruse to delay the proceedings indefinitely.

So the trial continued and Koch had the audacity to say: "It is only today from the indictment that I have learned about the terrible things which were done in Poland. As a German I wish to express my deep regret and my highest disgust at such happenings. I am completely shocked by what has been read here. I stand before this court and the Polish nation as a penitent for deeds committed by others. I am not guilty. The guilt lies with those who today are free, and I have been sent here while they remain free, as I might have been dangerous to them."

He claimed that he had always been a Socialist, had played a leading part in establishing the Soviet-Nazi Pact of 1939, and was known in the Nazi Party as its "Red Flag". Hitler had said to him: "You never were my friend, but I believe you will keep your oath. You are thought of as an extreme Socialist." He went on to argue that the British had handed him over to the Poles as an "act of revenge of a capitalist concern" because he had broken Unilever's virtual monopoly of margarine in Germany when he was reforming the East Prussian economy before the war.

His statements, so obviously aimed at pleasing his Marxist

judges, drew incredulous chuckles from the court. He spoke of his humble origins and of his association with "Papa Schmitz" a revered Social Democratic coalminer who, he said, had first opened his eyes to the verities of Marx, Engels, Lassalle and Bebel, names which he mentioned with reverence. This amounted to a claim that he was a Communist, and he followed it by telling the court that not only should it acquit him but also that it should express its appreciation of the work he had done in averting the worst German excesses in the Polish provinces under his administration. He described himself as "the only one to fight against the current" of Himmler's resettlement and extermination policies in this part of Europe.

Not surprisingly, his arguments could not stand against the weight of the evidence and the witnesses who, one after the other, in tragic procession, told of his brutalities. On March 9th, 1959, ten years since the time of his arrest and after a trial lasting nearly five months, he was sentenced to death. The sentence was greeted with applause.

But now the mystery begins. One year later it was announced that, under Article 407 of the Polish penal code, which disallows the execution of seriously ill persons, Koch had been reprieved.

A spokesman for the War Crimes Commission attached to the Polish Ministry of Justice told the authors that the year's delay between the passing of the death sentence on Koch and its commutation was due to the "necessity for lengthy investigation". But what did these investigations aim to discover and what secrets did Koch trade?

To our surprise we discovered that Koch, now eighty-three years old, is still alive, looked after in a private and guarded ward in a prison hospital in Rakowiecka Street, Warsaw. The last of the master butchers of the Holocaust, the epitome of Nazi evil, he must look back on the scenes at the burning dock at Pillau and his survival since 1945 as something of a triumph. That is, if he can live with his conscience.

There is still another mystery concerning Koch – a mystery which seems to link him with the *Wilhelm Gustloff*. It is known that in the last days before his flight, Koch was busy with an enterprise which was in accord with his eventual criminality: an enterprise concerning a unique and priceless horde of amber. To explain the nature of this treasure trove, it is necessary to delve back over two and a half centuries into history.

Amber, the fossil resin from now extinct coniferous trees, is found mainly along the Baltic coast of Germany, Lithuania and Latvia, and one of the chief sources is a mine at Palmnicken in what is now East Germany. It was already being made into jewellery in the Bronze Age and the Greeks and Romans prized it, using it mainly in small pieces of decorative work.

But King Frederick I of Prussia did not believe in small pieces. He panelled a whole room in amber. Completed in 1709 by the architect Schlutter and the jeweller Gottfried Tusso, the decoration consisted of fifty-five square metres of beautifully carved panelling. The panels were set in polished mosaic and decorated with landscapes, coats of arms and monograms, shells and garlands. Spaced among them were smaller plates of amber inlaid with miniatures of extraordinary detail, so small that they needed a magnifying glass to be studied properly. Silver foil laid on the back of the transparent plates showed off the effect of the light.

It was a beautiful piece of work which almost ruined the finances of the State of Prussia, and Frederick showed it off proudly to his visitors. But his son, Frederick William I, virtual founder of the Prussian Army, was more interested in six-foot-tall soldiers. So when Peter the Great of Russia visited him at his Potsdam palace in 1716 and admired the amber room, the Prussian king struck a bargain with him. He could have the amber in exchange for sixty giants from the Tsar's Imperial Guard.

The amber panels were dismantled and carried by sleigh to

Peter's Winter Palace at St. Petersburg, now Leningrad. After his death his daughter, the fiercely anti-German Tsarina Elizabeth, had it moved to the summer palace at Tsarkoye Selo, outside the city. There, because the room where she wanted the panels installed was larger than the original rooms, she brought in the amber jeweller Martelli to fill in the gaps. He did this brilliantly, mounting mirrors on white and gold tables between the panels and using gilded lighting fixtures to bring out the detail of the relief work.

The finished room was of a stunning beauty. Teams of men were trained to clean and polish the panels and the room was known as the "poem in amber". After the revolution in 1917 the room was opened to the public and its fame spread world wide.

But in 1941, with the Germans advancing on Leningrad, preparations were made to ship it to the safety of under-ground vaults in Sverdlovsk in the Urals. But the Russians were too late. They got two trainloads of treasures safely away but the Amber Room itself was not dismantled in time and it fell into the greedy hands of Erich Koch. He had it shipped to Königsberg early in 1942 where it was set up and restored by Dr. Alfred Rohde, director of the Prussian Fine Arts Museum and one of the world's leading authorities on amber. Koch then issued orders that entry to the room should be restricted. But one man who was allowed to see the room in the summer of 1943 reported: "The panels seemed in almost perfect condition. On entering, I was given a booklet which related the long history of the Amber Room, claiming that it was, properly speaking, a German possession, now at last restored to its rightful owners." But by the end of 1943, Bomber Command had started to pay attention to Königsberg, so Rohde dismantled the Amber Room and stored the panels in a cellar.

He regarded this as a temporary measure but eventually he was ordered to load the amber into twenty-four strongboxes suitable for "long transportation". In a note dated January

12th, 1945, eighteen days before the *Wilhelm Gustloff* sailed, he wrote: "I am packing the Amber Study in boxes and other containers on the orders of the provincial custodian. As soon as this is done, I shall evacuate the panels to Wechselburg, near Rochlitz in Saxony."

The packing was completed on January 15th and the strongboxes were piled in the castle yard. And from that moment all trace of the contents of the Amber Room has vanished.

The amber did not arrive in Wechselburg. Rohde and his wife died mysteriously in late 1945, leaving no indication of what had happened to it. Some think that it was buried in the cellars of Königsberg Castle, or in a bunker which has now been built over. Others believe it lies 2,145 feet down a flooded salt mine near the West German university town of Göttingen.

Dr. Georg Stein, who devotes himself to recovering treasures looted by the Germans during the war, is a supporter of the salt-mine theory. His evidence is a coded telex message sent to Berlin in January 1945 and signed "Ringel, SS Group North–East Königsberg, Prussia". It says: "Amber Room, operation completed, object is stored in B. Sch. W.V." Stein thinks this refers to B Shaft at a salt mine twelve miles from Göttingen known as Wittekind Vollprie-hausen – the W.V. of the coded telex. Nobody has been able to test this theory because the mine was flooded after an explosion in September 1945, when it was being used as a dump for unwanted ammunition by the British Army.

But there is another explanation of the coded telex. "Sch." is not only short for shaft. It is also short for "Schiffsraum", or hold. Therefore, accepting that there could have been a substitution of one letter, V for G, in the coding, the message could have meant: "Object is stored in B Hold on the *Wilhelm Gustloff*."

Nobody can prove that the Amber Room is lying at the bottom of the Baltic. It is certain, however, that the last time it was seen was in the castle yard a few days before the *Wilhelm Gustloff* sailed. We know that Erich Koch was desperately anxious to keep it out of Russian hands – he despatched a Field Marshal to escort it from Leningrad. And we know that nobody has admitted seeing it since the liner went down.

The Russians searched for the amber after the war and found no trace of it. Some years ago there were reports that the Poles, believing that it had been put on the *Wilhelm Gustloff* – which rests in Polish waters – were thinking of mounting an underwater expedition to find it. But no serious exploration of the wreck appears to have been carried out. The fate of the Amber Room, one of the world's most extraordinary works of art, remains a mystery.

Bibliography

Amalrik, Andrei, *Involuntary Journey to Siberia*, Collins & Harvill, London 1970

Archives of *Ostpreussenblattes*, Hamburg

Bekker, Cajus, *Flucht übers Meer*, Ullstein Buch, Frankfurt 1976

Bagramyan, Marshal Ivan, *How we Advanced to Victory*, Voenizdat, Moscow 1978

Brassey's Naval Annual, *Führer Naval Conference 1939-45*, H.M. Stationery Office

Breyer, Siegfried, *Guide to the Soviet Navy*, US Naval Inst., 1970

Brustat-Naval, Fritz, *Unternehmen Rettung*, Koehler Verlagsgesellschaft, Herford

Churchill, Winston S., *The Second World War*, Vol VI, *Triumph and Tragedy*, Cassell & Co, London 1954

Cookridge, E. H., *Gehlen, Spy of the Century*, Hodder and Stoughton, London 1971

Conquest, Robert, *Kolyma, The Arctic Death Camps*, Macmillan, London 1978

Dmitriyev, Captain Vasily, *Submarines Attack*, Voenizdat, Moscow 1964

Doenitz, Karl, *Deutsche Strategie zur See im Zweiten Weltkrieg*, Bernard & Graefe, Frankfurt 1972

—— *Memoirs, Ten Years and Twenty Days*, Weidenfeld & Nicolson, London 1959

Dunnigan, James F., *The Russian Front*, Arms & Armour Press, London 1978

Erickson, John, *The Soviet High Command*, Macmillan, London 1962

Fredmann, Ernst, *Sie Kamen übers Meer*, SWG, Cologne 1971

Gehlen, General Reinhard, *The Gehlen Memoirs*, Collins, London 1972

Germanov, Victor, *The Feat of the S 13*, Kaliningrad Publishing House, Kaliningrad 1970

Golovko, Admiral A. G., *Together with the Fleet*, Voenizdat, Moscow 1960

Great March of Liberation, The, Progress Publishing House, Moscow 1972

Grishchenko, Captain P. D., *My Friends the Submariners*, Lenizdat, Leningrad 1966

Hezlet, Arthur, *The Submarine and Sea Power*, Peter Davies, London 1967

Jackson, Robert, *The Red Falcons*, Clifton Books, London 1970

History of the Great Patriotic War of the Soviet Union (1941-45), Ministry of Defence Publishing House, Moscow 1963

Khrushchev, Nikita, *Khrushchev Remembers*, André Deutsch, London 1971

Kopelev, Lev, *No Jail for Thought*, Secker & Warburg, London 1977

Kron, Alexander and others, *Alongside the Heroes*, Writers Union, Moscow 1967

Lass, Edgar Gunther, *Die Flucht, Ostpreussen 1944-45*, Podzun-Verlag, Bad Nauheim, 1964

Lehndorf, Count Hans von, *East Prussian Diary, A Journal of Faith 1945-47*, Oswald Wolff, London 1963

Liddel Hart, Capt. Basil, *The Soviet Army*, Weidenfeld & Nicolson, London 1956

Medvedev, Roy, *Let History Judge*, Alfred A. Knopf Inc., USA 1971

Meister, Jurg, *Soviet Warships of the Second World War*, Macdonald & Jane's Ltd, London 1977

Mielke, Otto, *Katastrophe bei Nacht*, Arthur Moewig Verlag, Munich

Montgomery, Field Marshal, The Viscount, *Normandy to the Baltic*, Hutchinson, 1947

Porten, Edward P. von der, *The German Navy in World War Two*, Pan Books, London 1970

Red Flag Baltic Fleet in the Decisive Period of the Great Patriotic War, 1944-45, Nauka Publishing House, Moscow 1975.

Rohwer, J. & Hummelchen G., *Chronology of the War at Sea 1939-45*, (Two Vols), Military Book Society, London 1972

Sajer, Guy, *The Forgotten Soldier*, Ballantine Books, Harper & Row, USA 1971

Schapiro, Leonard, *The Communist Party of the Soviet Union*, Random House, USA 1959

Schoen, Heinz, *Untergang die Wilhelm Gustloff*, Pabel Taschenbuch, Baden 1960

Seaton, Albert, *The Russo-German War 1941-45*, Arthur Barker, London

Sellwood, A. V., *The Damned Don't Drown*, Tandem, London 1974

Shtemenko, General Sergei, *The Soviet General Staff at War*, Progress Publishing, Moscow 1975
Smirnov, Admiral Nikolai, *Sailors Defend the Motherland*, Politizdat, Moscow 1973
—— *Notes of a Member of the Military Council*, Politizdat, Moscow 1973
Solzhenitsyn, Alexander, *Prussian Nights*, Collins & Harvill Press, London 1977
—— *The Gulag Archipelago*, William Collins Sons & Co, Glasgow 1974
Showell, J. P. Mallman, *Boats under the Swastika*, Ian Allen, London 1973
Thorwald Jurgen, *Flight in Winter*, Pantheon Books. New York 1951
Toland, John, *The Last 100 Days*, Random House, USA 1965
Travkin, Captain Ivan, *Contempt for Death*, Voenizdat, Moscow 1976
Tuchman, Barbara W., *The Guns of August*, Dell Publishing, USA 1962
Whiting, Charles, *Finale at Flensburg*, Leo Cooper, London 1973
Worth, Alexander, *Russia at War*
Zayas, Alfred M. de, *Nemesis at Potsdam*, Routledge & Kegan Paul, London 1977

Also *Pravda, Izvestia, Komsomolskaya Pravda, Krasnaya Zvezda, Literaturnaya Gazeta, Vecherni Leningrad*, and other Soviet newspapers. Soviet Magazines with articles on the incidents included *Neva Zvezda, Molodoi Kommunist, Morskoi Flot, Vodnoi Transport, Moryak Odessa*, etc.

Index

213

216

217

219